Ackee and Roti

Narinder Kaur Purewal

Disclaimer

I have tried to recreate events and conversations from my memory of them. To protect the privacy in some instances I have changed the names of individuals.

Dedication

To our children Rijkaard, Jeevan, Khula, Shanae and Aveer.

To our dear grandparents and families in India, currently taking part in the biggest protest of the 21st Century, 'The Farmer's Protest,' we stand with you.

Acknowledgement

I will start by acknowledging my ancestors for guiding me throughout my life. Our brother, who didn't make it to this earthly plane but helped bring me here so that I could experience life.

Thank you to my Baba Ji, Maa Ji, and Papa Ji. My dear father-in-law, Jeevan, and Shanae's grandad.

I thank my Dad for letting me live my life and allowing me to have the freedom to explore the world we live in. My dad was and will always be my hero. Thank you for permitting me to write about my life's journey and experiences.

I thank my mum for being my best friend and raising me to be a strong mum just like her.

I thank my brother and sister for always being by my side and never allowing anyone or anything to break the special bond that we have had growing up. Thank you to Cassian and his family for bringing love, laughter, and joy into Jeevan and Shanae's lives and for showing unconditional love for them. I couldn't have picked a better family to help raise them in.

Thank you to my children Jeevan and Shanae, for supporting me and understanding why it was important for me to share a part of our journey with the world. This book is my legacy to both of you, and I hope that you can both appreciate how important living a truthful life is.

I wrote this book straight from my heart and therefore knew that I would need to get my soul tribe to help support me through some of the difficult chapters of this book.

I want to thank my dear friend Nathan and his wife, Phoebe. They have shown me immense support during my writing process and encouraged me to keep going, especially when I felt like giving up. Their advice and some of the conversations we have had around some of the topics covered in this book have been invaluable.

I would like to thank my soul sister, Michelle. You were the first forever friend I made in my early childhood days. I remember that day very clearly when you approached me and asked me to come to the shops with you. Neither of us cared what skin colour we were or what our religion was. We just saw one another as people. How have you and I never had a falling out in our lives? That is a miracle in itself!

My dear friend, who I call sister Manni, also known as Jeevan, and Shanae's Massi Ji. Your support not just throughout this writing process but through some of my darkest days has helped me move forward and not look back. You have treated Jeevan and Shanae as your own children and given them so much love and care that they see you in a motherly way. The fact that Jeevan says your *rotis* are better than mine says it all.

Without you, I could never have written this book. I wrote most of this book without Jeevan and Shanae around me, so thank you for taking care of them during this time and understanding that I needed to be alone to write the way I have. Thank you for always just being real with me and straight-up honest too.

Thank you to another soul sister of mine, Shantyl,

who lifted me up when I was feeling a little anxious about writing about some of my personal experiences. One morning, we were both up with the sunrise. I was sitting in the garden just listening to the birds feeling happy and blessed, appreciating everything around me; I messaged Shantyl and asked her to send out some good vibes for me to the universe regarding Ackee and Roti. She replied, *"I'm on it, sis, you're a teacher, so now go teach."* She sent me some inspirational music too and said that she was also up early listening to the birds and that maybe her birds knew my birds.

A big thank you to my cousin Jindy who read each chapter as I completed it and gave me feedback. There were times she would get upset because she wasn't aware of my darkest days. Jindy is younger than me, and she said to me, *"I wish I had been older at that time, then I could have been there for you."* But I told her that sometimes, you have to go through things alone without anyone's support. This is how you find your inner strength.

I thank my Massi Ji for being a true inspiration for

me throughout my whole life.

I would also like to thank Tobias, Salma, Ramona, Siobhan, Stacey, Janine, Lee-Ann, Sati, Pat, Kully, June, and Alan.

And finally, I thank myself for never giving up and finding my inner strength to create the best version of myself.

CONTENTS

About the Author

Narinder Kaur Purewal is a single mother to her two children Jeevan and Shanae. After working in secondary mainstream schools for 16 years and qualifying as a maths teacher, she now works in a Special Educational Needs school that specialises in Autism Spectrum Conditions or an identified social, emotional, or mental health need.

Preface

My name is Narinder Purewal, and I am a forty-one-year-old woman. Despite having spent only four short decades in this life, it often feels like I have been living forever. I am currently sitting in my garden, watching the beautiful, dark sky and anticipating that it will rain soon.

The rain makes me feel happy. It has become almost habitual for me to sit here while reflecting on my life's struggles. Over the years, I have often discussed them with my friends, and they have consistently encouraged me to pen down all my thoughts. And finally, it feels like the penny has dropped. That is the very reason I am sitting here today.

I was asking myself - What is stopping me from writing everything down and sharing it with the world?

And asking you - Have you ever felt like you didn't know who you were and where you fit in society?

This is an original story about my life. There's a part of me that has always wanted to share my struggles with others. There is so much going on in my mind. I want to be a source of motivation for anyone going through difficult times, much like the ones I have experienced.

The problems that I've faced have made me stronger. If anyone is going through a rough patch (or patches!), as I did, I'd like to say, "hang on." Believing the statement "life gets better" may seem hard and somewhat cliché, but trust me, life does get better. In this book, I want to take you with me on a journey throughout my life – You'll read about my experiences of being a British Punjabi growing up in Coventry. You'll read about my relationships and how the *ackee* and the *roti* came together to create the title of this book.

You'll see how my personality developed over time, how I learnt to master the art of patience and how NOT to judge a book by its cover. I am not perfect, and I didn't always get it right, but I will be as honest as I can on these pages and tell you everything. You will see that I learnt not to care about where somebody is from if they have a different culture, religion, or identity, but to focus on whether they are good people with good hearts. I learnt to accept people the way they are.

As I take out my favourite pen and diary and start to jot everything down, my heart relaxes. As the words keep flowing out of me, I feel calmer and happier. I know I am doing the right thing. I'll be so proud of myself after writing this book. It is a labour of love and a testament to the kind of person I have become now. Before this day, I was always scared to say anything. But now, it feels like all the chains that bound me and held me back have been broken.

Today, I feel free to share my experiences with other people to let them know that they're not alone. So, let's start from the very beginning.

Chapter 1

The Beginning

*** MY CHILDHOOD ***

I came into this world in January of 1980, and I was a healthy baby, easily weighing 5 pounds. I came with a twin brother. Sadly, he passed away a few hours later due to complications.

Due to the complicated birth, my mum's health was poor, and both my parents were also sad about my brother's death. However, the moment was bittersweet for them because they were also happy that I had survived.

My mum was kept in the hospital for a while longer after my birth. During that time, I was sent to live with my mum's parents, whom I called Maa Ji and Papa Ji. (In the Indian culture, we add the word 'Ji' at the end of someone's name to show respect, and it is commonly used to show reverence to our elders). They took good care of me, and I guess my closeness to my grandparents stemmed from here.

My mum told me that I gave her the sweetest smile when she held me in her arms, a smile that was unblemished by the hurts of life. My little face had glowed from a light within, and it felt like it was my destiny to live an extraordinary life, one that would be free from difficulties. But boy, was I wrong.

A few weeks later, when my mum came home from the hospital, I went back home to live with my parents. I also met my brother Manbiar, who was a year older than me. Whenever I cried, my mum calmed me down by singing lullabies, and she stroked my tiny back and soft hair. I loved hearing her voice and being near her.

It made me feel safe, and I knew that the world would not hurt me if I had her by my side. I was always a sensitive child, and it took no time for me to burst into tears over the simplest of things.

A year later, after my birth, my sister Nicky was born, so there were three of us now. As I started growing up,

I noticed that my dad would work a lot. He had a job at the *Ford Motor Foundry*. While he was at work, my mum would take care of us.

My mum was young and vibrant, and she had lots of friends and family on the street that we lived on. She would always have get-togethers at the house. I vividly remember dancing a lot to *Bhangra* at these events. They were always musical, lively, and filled our house with laughter.

My mum loved to dance, and I believe that I have inherited this trait from her. I grew up mainly speaking Punjabi in the household. It wasn't until I started school that I learnt how to speak English fluently at the age of five.

As a child, I would always be with my brother and sister, and no matter what, we would have fun. We had a splendid time together, and I always felt like myself with them. My siblings are my pillars. They have supported me in every decision I have made. I can say that not many people are blessed with such good siblings, but fortunately, I was.

When it came to birthdays, I was also lucky. Our birthdays got celebrated to the fullest in my family. It just so happened that my brother and I were birthday twins, and we would get to cut the same birthday cake. Everyone celebrated our birthdays together, and it would turn into a huge celebration. My mum would dress my brother and me in matching clothes too. I think she did this because her son, my twin, she had lost, and as my brother and I were only a year apart, we could get away with looking like twins. Until my sister came along, she would dress my sister and me the same as if we were twins. So most of my baby pictures, I am either dressed like my brother or like my sister.

I can remember that we would get one toy each on our birthday as a present. It meant so much to me at the time, and I never felt like I wanted more. A cake and a special present were all that was needed to make me happy.

That one toy was enough for me. I would usually get a doll or a new teddy bear, which I would then cling onto until the next birthday. Since we would be celebrating two birthdays together, it would be a big event. Everybody gathered on our birthdays at our place, and my mum would often spend the entire day making *samosas* and *pakoras* for the guests.

I grew up in a very Punjabi household that was very welcoming to others. People would always come over to our house. We used to throw big feasts for the family, and since we are Punjabis, we loved eating. Our most favourite food item was *butter chicken*.

The juicy chicken pieces were cooked to perfection, bathed in a creamy, flavourful gravy, and were just bursting with flavour. We paired it up with some freshly made *naan* or *rotis*. It stole our hearts away every time we ate it.

I can proudly say that many of the neighbours were also a fan of our homemade *butter chicken*. My family would usually throw a Saturday-night party, and everyone was invited. People usually came to have a good gossip session and to eat some delicious food.

We lived with our dad's uncle in Radford in Coventry, whom we called *Baba Ji*. He was very dear to us. Together, we lived in a small house that was bright and colourful, and a Pakistani family lived next door to us.

They greeted us politely every time they saw us. We often played with their children and ate together. I remember that we would walk in and out of each other's houses and shared the sorrows and joys of our lives together like we were one big family.

We didn't have much of a garden, but they did, and they would always let us play there. I remember them saying, *"Our garden is your garden too."*

Although our house was small, the size of the house never seemed like a problem to us. We adjusted to it, no matter what, and even when parties were held, there was always room for everyone there. All our cousins gathered at Baba Ji's place, and we had a perfect time. He took care of us like we were his own children. His personality was one-of-a-kind, and he was a *giver* more than a *taker*.

He would always have milky bar chocolates ready for the three of us, and we would wait each day for our milky bar. I remember that we even found his secret stash – a box full of milky bars, but we never took them without his permission. Instead, we were very patient, as we knew that we would get one anyway. I remember he would take us out for walks, and I would hold onto his finger and skip alongside him.

Unfortunately, Baba Ji passed away when I was only seven years old. It was a devastating moment for the whole family and me as well. I remember the day that he died. He was sleeping on the sofa peacefully, and my mum was trying to wake him up. Despite her calls to wake up, he didn't move.

My siblings and I were playing and running around the house, and I remember that we stopped and ran to see what the commotion was. My mum was struggling to hold back tears as she kept asking him to wake up. We stared at him, waiting for him to move, but he didn't, even when my mum was pleading with him. That's when my heart sank, tears rolled down my eyes, I felt a knot in my stomach, and that's when I knew.

An ambulance arrived, and the three of us were left at our neighbour's house by my mum. We saw that people started visiting the house regularly, and a white sheet was spread on the floor. In our culture, when someone dies, a white sheet is placed on the floor, and the home is transformed into a mourning room. People came to pray and offer condolences for Baba Ji. We weren't allowed to run around the house anymore, and there was a sombre aura in the house.

After his death, we had to shift to a new home to Cheylesmore - a suburb in the southern half of Coventry. My parents showed us the house before they bought it. What's even more impressive is that they let us take part in picking the house.

Although, to be honest, we weren't very picky. Our criteria for any house was it should have a garden. With the house our parents showed to us, the three of us just ran straight to the garden and said, *"Can we have this house, please?"* The garden in this house was huge compared to our last house. Luckily, that house also met my parent's requirements. Not long after that, we were moving in.

We had much more space, and this time, we even had our very own playroom. By now, we had more toys than before, and we loved playing board games in the playroom. We could often spend hours there, sitting around the table, having a fun time as we tried to win. Most of our board games were hand-me-down pieces from our older cousins.

These usually came with missing game pieces, but we never complained about that. We would simply grab a marker and draw on the missing pieces of paper for games like *Monopoly* and *Scrabble*.

It can't be said that we played very reasonably or according to the rules. We would often get into silly arguments, especially if we lost; none of us liked losing one bit, and we were often sore losers too.

My parents would also try to spend time with us and take us to the park. My dad would make sure he had taken a bag of Bombay mix and some drinks for us if we got hungry. On some occasions, my mum would take us fishing. We never caught any fish, but we would get excited because we had rods.

Both my parents worked in shifts now, so at times they didn't even get to see each other. My dad would work nights and sleep during the day, and my mum would work during the day and be home at night with us. We spent the weekends with our cousins, aunties, and uncles in the house, watching TV, talking, and eating together.

I lived a peaceful life in our home in Cheylesmore. The activity in the place would often ebb and flow like the tide. There would be times when the place remained quiet sometimes, while there was quite a rush at other times. It was all good because my family was there.

We lived near the train station, and my room, which I shared with my sister, was at the back of the house near the tracks. It was noisy, especially when a train was passing by. I remember the first few times it happened; I nearly jumped out of my skin. It gave me a huge fright. But eventually, I got used to knowing when the next train was going by. I loved watching the trains, and I would always take some time out to watch them pass.

We had friendly neighbours in the new place, and we were fortunate. We got along with them pretty well. We lived next door to a Gujarati family, and whenever we cooked anything delicious in our home, we sent it out to them, and they would do the same. This was done as a gesture of kindness, and everyone acknowledged each other's efforts. On the other side was an English family who was also very friendly.

As I mentioned earlier, I belong to the Punjabi culture. You might have an image of it in your mind, but it is not how it is shown in Bollywood movies. Real-life is somewhat different than what they are showing on the screen. One thing that they do get right and which you need to know about Punjabis is that we are loud.

Punjabis also have the biggest heart. You can come to us with any problem, and we would find a solution for it. We are very welcoming, and our guests never leave our house without a smile on their faces.

Sharing is also one of the best qualities about us. We'll gladly beckon you with *"Ao Ji, saade naal khaao ji,"* which means, *"Come, eat with us,"* in English. We do not like to show off either; we are generous yet humble.

I made my first new friend called Michelle at the age

of eight when we moved to Cheylesmore. She lived around the corner from me. She was English, had beautiful brown hair, and she had the most honest face too.

My siblings and I were only allowed to play on the drive at the front of the garden, and that was where I met Michelle. She was also the same age as me. She had asked me if I had wanted to come to the local shop and get the bread with her. Her mum had asked her to do so. I said I needed to ask my mum first before I could accompany her.

At first, my mum said no. However, when I called Michelle into the house to meet my mum, I was permitted to accompany her. The shop was only a short walk from our homes, and we were back in no time.

After that, we played outside often. As our friendship became stronger, I would go over to her house, and she would come over to mine. Michelle lived with her parents and her big sister. Her parents reminded me of my own parents. Her mum always looked so glamorous, and her dad was soft-natured like mine. We made it a habit to eat at each other's homes. My parents would make a different curry every day, and the food was always delicious.

Michelle always wanted to come over and eat with us. She loved my mum's *'saag'* and *rotis* the most. I also went over to her house frequently and ate English food with her family. We didn't have much English food at our house. I would often get sick of eating *roti* every day.

As our friendship grew stronger, we also ended up going to the same secondary school. Another happy coincidence was that we were also in the same class. We would then walk to school and walk back home together as well.

I was never allowed out late, though, while Michelle was, which often frustrated me. However, I never quarrelled about it with my parents, as I was very young. Even at that age, I knew that there would be no way that my parents would allow me out late.

Chapter 2

Mixed Cultures

My parents had brought diverse cultures into our household. My mum's mother, who we called Maa Ji, was a Malaysian Hindu.

My mum's father, who we called Papa Ji, was a Punjabi Sikh from India. Papa Ji had left India when the partition happened, and he had moved to Malaysia.

The partition of India was a challenging time for everyone. It was an event that triggered one of the bloodiest upheavals in human history. Around 14 million people abandoned their homes in the summer and fall of 1947 when the British colonial administration started dividing India in South East Asia.

While the aim had been to have a peaceful partition, the people's animosity and bitterness led to a lot of bloodshed. The estimated number of people killed in those months' ranges between 200,000 and 2 million. A massive amount of people moved to what they had hoped would be a safer place, Pakistan. However, many chose to head to other places.

It was a completely new country for him, and he was clueless for quite a few days. He wanted to find a respectful family from whom he could take help. That is when he met Maa Ji's family there, and they treated him with respect and as one of their own.

Maa Ji took care of him and made him feel less lonely in this new country. The partition had been very hard for him. However, he fell in love with my grandmother, and so did she. They both came from different backgrounds.

Regardless of this, they got married after a few months of knowing each other and lived a happy and complete life. They got along so well and could not imagine a day without each other. It took them some time to adjust to living together, but they eventually did it with success. They started a new life in Malaysia. One day, Papa Ji received news that he had been granted permission to come to the United Kingdom - this was when the British were allowing immigrants into the country for work purposes. This meant that my mum was brought to England when she was only 12 months old. They settled in Royal Leamington Spa - and she went to school there.

My dad came over from India to England. It was here that he had a marriage arranged for him to my mum. Papa Ji was a strict Punjabi Sikh, and as soon as my mum turned sixteen, he arranged to have her married to my dad.

Before the marriage, my parents had only seen pictures of each other. They met for the first time at the airport with their families when my dad arrived.

My dad's family were farmers in India and originally came from the city of Lahore, now in Pakistan's Punjab Province. However, after the partition, they were uprooted from Lahore and moved to Punjab, a state in India. Here they bought land and continued the farming trade. My dad's father died when he was only seven years old, and his mother died when he was only eleven years old. My dad was then raised by his brothers, sisters, and his sisters-in-law.

My mum was only sixteen years old when she got married to my dad. It was hard for her to manage everything at such a young age, but she knew she had to do it. It was considered better in our culture to get married early. She went through many troubles, but she was a strong lady.

My mum had all of her children by the age of twenty. She wanted to contribute to the household, so she started working.

Living in a Punjabi household was very entertaining for us. There were many relatives I didn't even know the real names of. I had always heard people calling them *"Bobby,"* *"Pinky,"* *"Tony."* I bet that they might have gotten so used to being called by those names that they may have forgotten their real names.

The nickname that my dad gave me was *'Bubbly.'* To this day, I have never heard my parents or other family members call me by my full name. I am always known as *'Bubbly'* to them. Close friends and cousins also call me by that nickname.

However, being in a Punjabi household came with a lot of criticism and racism, especially from the outside world. People would often call us *"Paki,"* and told us to go back to our own country, which often hurt. My mum did her best to protect me from racism, and I was grateful to her. Otherwise, I would've been scarred by it.

My appearance was not of a 'typical' Indian girl while growing up. I had inherited Maa Ji's curly hair and almond-shaped eyes and my dad's brown eye colour. I was also slightly plump compared to my sister, who had straight hair and was skinny. At the time, I wished my hair was straight like my sister's. My hair would always be bushy even after I combed it.

Both my sister and I had hair that went below our backs. Mum eventually let us cut our hair when I was fourteen years old. She sent us to the hairdressers to get a little trim, but I persuaded my sister to cut it to our shoulders. I was desperate to have hair like some of the girls in my school and didn't care what mum would say at that time. Cutting my hair seemed more important to me.

My mum was furious with us when we got back, and I remember her exclaiming, *"Wait till your dad gets back from work and sees your hair!"* My sister and I spent the evening waiting for dad to get back, frightened we were going to get into big trouble. My sister was more upset than I was as she had got the main brunt of our mum's anger. When dad came in, mum showed him what we had done, and his reply to mum was, *"Well, what did you expect? You cut your hair, so they wanted to be like you."*

My dad never shouted at my sister or me. He was always so gentle and kind when it came to us, whereas with my brother, he would tell him off if he had done something he shouldn't have. My mum was the opposite; she would tell my sister and me off but not my brother. We always felt that was unfair, and I know my brother felt like that towards our dad. My dad didn't speak English fluently, so our conversations were always in Punjabi with him. We became good at translating from Punjabi to English and vice versa because of this.

The girls in our family got married at an early age, so

most of my cousins got married young. Punjabi weddings are highly entertaining. I remember we all used to go daily to the bride's house at least a few months before her wedding and discuss the clothes we were going to wear. We had different designs in mind for our *salwar kameez,* a traditional outfit worn by Punjabi women. It consists of a pair of trousers called "salwar" and a tunic called "kameez." When they got stitched, they looked even more beautiful than we'd imagined.

The best part about Punjabi weddings was the loud music and delicious food. From the spicy *tandoori chicken* to the creamy *palak paneer* and the soft and sweet *gulab jamun*, everything was scrumptious. The *tandoori chicken* was the family favourite. It was roasted and marinated with yoghurt and spices perfectly. And of course, we loved desserts, so when *gulab jamun* was served, our hearts danced with happiness.

During these years, we attended many family weddings, and it felt like someone was getting married every weekend. Punjabi weddings also lasted for three days. We enjoyed these family events and caught up with our cousins.

I was familiar with the Sikh Gurdwara, as I would always go with my family. I loved eating the *parshad* and *Kheer* when it was time for *'langar'* (free food served at the Gurdwara). I would always feel mesmerized by the bride and groom. I loved the bride's outfits; they were so colourful, and she'd look like a princess. One day, I thought that would be me.

We would wear beautiful Punjabi suits for weddings, one for each of the three days. Sometimes my mum would make them for us because she was taught how to stitch and make salwar kameez when she was young. That was the primary skill of most Indian women; to know how to stitch clothes.

The wedding parties were the main event, as I loved dancing to the *dhol* and *Bhangra* songs. Aunties would always grab the young girls to start dancing first. I guess that way, they didn't feel embarrassed coming onto the stage next. My sister would be a little shy, but I, on the other hand, didn't need to be told twice.

The only part of the wedding I disliked was when my dad would get drunk with my uncles and be one of the last people to leave. My mum would spend ages trying to get him to go home. She would ask the three of us to go and get him, and he would always ask her to wait for five more minutes, but his five more minutes were like two hours. Even then, he would be staggering home and on repeat with telling us about his life in India and how he missed his parents, and the hardships he had been through. We would listen attentively and feel sad for him.

My dad worked very hard, and when it came to such events, he would indulge in drinking full bottles of Bells Whiskey, Bacardi, beers, and eating. My dad spent most Friday and Saturday evenings drinking at home, cooking delicious lamb or chicken curry, either watching Punjabi films or listening to old Punjabi folk music. He rarely went out with friends to the pub; the only time he would go to the pub was when his family was visiting, and it was almost a custom that the women would stay home and cook, and the men went to the pub.

When they got back, the women would feed the men and children first, and then they would sit down, eat and clean up after. I used to feel for my mum, as she seemed to do most of the work all day when visitors were coming over.

As I grew older, I was expected to help and make Indian tea for the guests. My hands would shake, bringing in the tea as I knew everyone was watching me, and I would wait for the verdict on my tea. It was either too dark or too milky or would not have enough *'lenchi'* in it.

I did get better each time, though, and can now safely say that my Indian tea is delicious. Because I was the oldest daughter, my sister got away with making tea and dishing out food. I learnt to make *roti* and *curry* by just watching my parents cook.

The first time I made *roti*, my dad had said he would eat as many as it took for me to get my *roti* round and cooked properly. It took me nine *rotis* to get it right, and my dad ate every single one. Some were burnt, some were uncooked, and eight of them were not round, but on that ninth *roti*, my dad said to me, *"Bubbly, you did it."* He said it doesn't matter if the *roti* wasn't round. What matters is it is cooked properly.

I used to love watching Bollywood movies too and learnt how to speak and understand Hindi because of them. I didn't think it was much different from Punjabi. I would learn all the words to the songs and sing with my high-pitched voice, imagining myself as the actress. I would get up and dance around too. I loved Saturdays as my dad would take me to the Indian movie shop and let me pick the films.

The movies had similar storylines where there was a damsel in distress, and a man comes to save her, and then they fall in love, only to find out later their families have some sort of feud from the past so they can't be together. After lots of devastating events, the lovers would eventually get together, live a happy life, and the families would make up. There was always a happy ending, which is what I was drawn to.

I used to think this was what life would be like, and everyone would get a happy ending. Looking back now, I know that this is not always the case, and most movies were not a real perception of what life is about. But I learnt to believe in love during this time of my life; these movies gave me a sense of happiness and increased my belief in happily ever after.

My mum's younger brother and sister, who we called Mamma Ji and Massi Ji, would be over often too, and I would watch English movies with them. They were first-generation Indians like my siblings and me, and we got on well with them. One of my elder Mamma Jis had married an English woman, and so I had mixed-race cousins too, which I thought was really cool. My Massi Ji was also married to an English man.

But Papa Ji was not happy about this as it caused him shame and embarrassment that his son and daughter had married *'Gore,'* the Punjabi word for white people. I would often witness him ignoring them at family gatherings, and it felt awkward. I loved Papa Ji very much and could also understand why he felt like this as my dad and his family were very similar, and interracial marriage was not something they agreed with.

Maa Ji was different. She would treat them with compassion and love, making them *roti* and curries, sitting and talking to them, and playing with their children. We were all the same to Maa Ji.

Punjabi culture dominated our household. But it was also fun to live in it. It completely groomed my personality, and I always admired how my elders greeted everyone with such warmth and how everyone lived with such peace and harmony. I always saw my mum wearing colourful *salwar kameez*, and I admired how she dressed. It's a pure indication of how bright and vibrant the Punjabi culture is.

My family strongly believed in the concept of arranged marriage and worked on finding suitable matches before the girl even completed her studies. Love marriages were hardly accepted. Even my mum and dad had an arranged marriage, so I could not even think of a love marriage at that time.

It scared me to think about my family's reaction if I ever wanted to have a love marriage. Their voices would get louder, and I would get a good scolding. I didn't want to imagine that situation.

Coming from the Sikh faith, I was taught about the Sikh Gurus, and we had pictures of the Gurus in our house. We attended the *Vaisakhi Mela* yearly, celebrated *Guru Nanak Dev Ji's* birthday, *Bandi Chor Divas,* and *Diwali* each year. We would attend the Gurdwara and set off fireworks in the garden. As Sikhs, we believed in Guru Nanak Dev Ji's teachings that there is only one God and that there was only one race, the human race. All humans were equal.

Our family consisted of many members, and our house was always crowded. People would come by to visit, and we thoroughly enjoyed it. The conversations were entertaining, and we laughed to the fullest. Time passed by quickly, and we never realised it.

Whenever someone from abroad was coming, they would stay at our house, and we would have a fantastic time together. We would feed them our most popular foods and take care of them properly. They'd get so attached to us that they would not want to leave. We treated our guests with care and kindness.

Living in a close-knit family helped us know about our family values and how to maintain them. We were close to our family and admired everyone. Whenever we would go to family weddings, our cars would be filled with people. And when it was time for the family photograph, it was hard to adjust the camera so that everyone could come into the frame.

Whenever we would have a feast at our place, our house would be jampacked. It would become hard to recognise our immediate family members because everyone looked alike. When the food would be served, everyone would go rushing to the table.

My whole family would gather for the festivals, and it was a wonderful time. We enjoyed it to a great extent, and no one slept the night before. We discussed the upcoming day the whole night and couldn't contain our excitement. The whole house was busy, and everybody ran here and there trying to find their clothes and ironing them.

When we got done with the clothes preparation, we started talking about the food. We decided on the whole menu the night before, and the next morning, the ladies of the house got up early so they could start making those dishes.

When we went away on day trips to the beach such as to 'Blackpool' and 'Great Yarmouth,' we would go with my aunties, uncles, and our cousins and squeeze into the car; my sister and I would usually have to sit in the boot so we could all fit. It used to be very uncomfortable. At that time, it was ok to have as many people in the car, and there were no laws in place regarding seat belts either.

I felt grateful to grow up in this family, and I will always be grateful for the many things it has taught me. I know that no matter where I'd go, I'd take all this along with me and never forget my culture. It is embedded in me now.

I will always talk about my culture with pride and I was extremely grateful to my family that they never let me forget about my values and taught me how to embrace them.

It genuinely made me a better person and made me think differently, and if you could hear my heart at that time, your ears would have been blessed by a happy song.

Chapter 3

Schooling

As I mentioned before, my siblings and I didn't start school until the age of five.

When my siblings and I did start at the local primary school, we thoroughly enjoyed it. The primary school we attended was a good mix of Indian, white, and black students, as the area we lived in was very diverse. We fitted in well and learnt to speak and read English fluently.

At the time, my mum played a big part in our primary school experience, she was on the PTA (parent-teacher association), and the teachers and other parents knew her well. She would organise many events with the other parents, such as Diwali plays and Christmas plays. Mum would dress me and my sister up for these plays, and I remember feeling embarrassed in my Punjabi suit, *bindi,* and ankle bracelets *(chanjur)*. She would walk us to school and pick us up too, and I have very fond memories of my first primary school and the teachers. The teachers were kind and caring.

When we left Radford and moved to Cheylesmore, we started school at the local primary. The area at the time was not as diverse as my old area. It was nicer and more middle class, though. We all settled in well, but we missed our old primary school. Here we were, the minority, but that didn't matter. We enjoyed our final years at primary and making new friends. We would walk to school by ourselves now, as both my parents would be at work. I noticed that the teachers here were much stricter too.

When it was time to start secondary school, we had the option of going on a bus or walking. Our dad would give us bus money, but we would choose to walk to school and spend it on sweets instead.

The secondary school my siblings and I attended was predominately white. When we first started there, it was common to be called '*Paki*' by some of the white children, especially if they decided they didn't like you, and it was like one of the first things they would say to us. I couldn't understand how just because we were different in colour gave them the right to call us racist names. I recall one day my sister and I were walking home and across the road, two other girls were walking home too, one of them shouted *'Paki'* at us, and we were shocked, as we hadn't even done anything. We decided to confront them, but they kept referring to us as *'Pakis.'* I recall saying we aren't even *'Pakistani'* and that they needed to educate themselves a little about where we actually came from. Anyway, we decided to walk away, and when we arrived home a short while later, my mum was upset as she had had a visit from the girls' mum, who had stated that my sister and I had been bullying her daughters on the way home.

We were clearly upset by this as that was not the case, and we told our mum what had really happened and that they had called us both *'Pakis'* first, that we were just trying to stick up for ourselves for a change. Luckily my mum understood, and nothing more was said about it. I was also able to tell my mum a few doors down our road a boy would always come up to me when I was outside the house and say, *'You Paki, go back to your own country.'* I would be sitting on my front wall, usually waiting for my friend Michelle to come over. He would see me and deliberately walk over and say that to me. He was a few years older than me, and I would just freeze; I would start shaking and hold my tears in. I would then run into the house and feel like I couldn't tell anyone as I may upset or ruin my parents' day, so I didn't bother until now. My mum just told me to ignore him.

I had made some friends at school now, and Michelle had also started school with me. We would spend a lot of our time together walking to and from school and in lessons all day. A few more Indian girls started school too in my class, but they were very competitive and always wanted to be the best in every subject. I think they had strict parents who put too much pressure on them to get the best grades. They were nice and friendly but getting good grades mattered to them more.

I wasn't too bothered about my grades. I just did the bare minimum. I was an average student, and my parents didn't really push us to study hard. They never checked if our homework was done; or attend our parents' evenings. Although they didn't play much of a part in encouraging us to do well, they would often say in conversation, *"You better do well at school if you want to go to college. We didn't get those opportunities, but you can."* I would only complete my homework because I had to; otherwise, my tutor would contact my parents. I didn't want to get into trouble at home.

As siblings, we stuck together when we were doing things we shouldn't have been. It was common to *'skip'* school, and I skipped school countless times with my friends. We would often skip our lessons to walk around the streets or go to the park before heading home. I got into the habit of forging my mum's signature too and writing notes to my teachers saying I had permission to leave early due to doctor's or dentist's appointments. I overdid it with my letters, though, and my mum found out when one of my teachers decided to keep them and send them to her. My mum confronted me about this. I felt upset more so because I had got caught, and my punishment was that I could not play out with my friends for a while.

My brother and sister would do the same thing and skip school too. Once we all decided to skip school and stay at home and then pretended to our parents, we had been to school all day. During our school days, the three of us started to cover for one another and not tell our parents about anything we were up to. We just had this imaginable agreement which we stuck by and knew how we had to be.

I would say that out of the three of us, I skipped school the most. But after this one incident, I learnt my lesson. When I started to get acne, I felt embarrassed about my appearance. My Massi Ji had told me she steamed her face when she was younger to get rid of spots, and that is how her skin cleared up. My Massi Ji was twelve years older than me, and she lived in London. She had somehow escaped the route of having an arranged married like my mum did and left Royal Leamington Spa. I admired and looked up to my Massi Ji. She was so beautiful too. Well, that day I skipped school, I thought I would steam my face, and my spots would disappear. So, I boiled the kettle and took the kettle to the bathroom, placing it on the toilet seat. Whilst I put the plug in the sink in that split second, the kettle fell to the floor, and the boiling water fell onto my feet. I screamed and ripped off my socks only to scream even more because I had seriously burnt my feet and ripped off a layer of my skin. I panicked and didn't even think to put my feet in cool water and just cried and screamed, watching my feet blister up. I was like this for around an hour before I had the courage to call my mum at work. I spent time weighing up the options; I thought I was definitely going to get into trouble for missing school, but I had no choice.

My mum came rushing home from work, and when she saw my feet, she called an ambulance. I was in shock by now and could barely speak to explain how it had happened. They stretchered me into an ambulance and bandaged up my feet; I was glad they didn't look a pretty sight at all. I was given medication to ease the pain. The police came to speak to me about what had happened. I think they thought maybe

I was being abused. I told them the truth about how I was trying to get rid of my acne and admitted skipping school. They checked that my mum was at work and that I had called her at work. My feet were burnt bad they had to pop my blisters, and that hurt. I had a nurse come to the house for the next two weeks to put fresh dressings on. My parents were just happy that I was ok and I don't recall them once shouting at me. I could see they were disappointed; that was easy to spot from their facial expressions. They were just grateful I was okay. My dad and mum would take turns to have days off to look after me at home as I couldn't walk. I still have those scars on my feet where I burnt them. My brother and sister were also concerned and would help me at home. I actually missed school during this time. I missed my friends the most, so I stopped skipping school after this.

During my final two years at school, I became more active in sports and joined the local cadets with my friends. I enjoyed the camping and training side of the cadets. We would wear an army uniform and go away for weekends camping, learning to cook for ourselves, reading maps, and navigating assault courses. We would have to get up early in the morning and start training around the field. I remember being tired and cold but having no choice but to join in; the Sergeants would shout at you if you didn't get up on time and make your beds, and that would be embarrassing. Once I took my teddies with me to the campsite and made my bed. The Sergeant came to inspect the dorms, and she asked, *"Whose bed is this?"* It was mine with at least six teddies on it. She made me take them down and pack them in my bag and told me never to bring any teddies again.

My punishment was to do extra laps around the field too. I was so embarrassed as all the other girls were laughing at me and saying that, *"She still sleeps with her teddies."* I still slept with my teddies and shared a bed with my sister, so I took them because I didn't want to feel lonely at bedtime. After that incident with my teddies, I stopped sleeping with them at home too. I felt maybe I needed to grow up now. I was the only Indian person in the group and endured racist comments from other children, again being called a *'Paki.'* My friends would stick up for me and tell the other children to go away and leave me alone. I felt very blessed that my friends treated me with respect and the same as others. I would never say anything back. I chose to ignore them, but my friends didn't like it and would cuss them back. I would get worried things would get worse, but they didn't. During this time, I also lost a lot of my puppy fat.

I had some wonderful friends at school. One of my friends was a West Indian boy called Nathan. He was in my class, and we would always be laughing and joking together. He was the class clown and popular amongst all the students. He would always make me laugh, and when I was around him, I would also become a bit of a clown too and start messing around trying to make others laugh. Once, I put a tampon we were given in sex education class in his school bag for a joke, and when he came in the next day, he said his mum, who also happened to be a maths teacher at our school, had found it and was not impressed. But he laughed about it and didn't get upset with me. On most occasions, we would be late for class and end up getting detention for it too. I lost count of how many detentions we got.

On the weekends, my siblings and I would have to accompany our parents to do the weekly shopping. Once we were in the supermarket and I saw Nathan shopping with his mum, he saw me, and I went over to talk to him. When I looked back, my parents were staring at me. I felt a little worried, thinking I may be in trouble, and told him I had to go. When I got home, my mum asked me who that boy was, and I told her he was my friend from school and that I was only saying hi. My mum said that it was not nice to walk away to talk to a boy and I had better not do that again. My dad didn't say anything. He just looked away from me as if he was ashamed of me. That was enough for me to know not to do that again. I couldn't help wondering, was it because it was a boy or because he was black?

During this time, some of my cousins had run away from home. One had run away with a Muslim boy, and she was only fifteen years old at the time. I recall being questioned by my parents, who wanted to know what I knew about it. A few weeks earlier, my cousin had come to stay with us and told my sister and me about her Muslim boyfriend. At that time, all of us girls used to write in our diaries, and her parents had read hers where she had written down how she had told my sister and me. We had no choice but to tell them what we knew. My parents were not happy with us, as we didn't tell them anything until she had run away. But it never occurred to me that we should tell them at the time. And if we had, we would have got her into trouble, and we didn't want that. After this, I tried to meet my cousin along with my sister, and we told her to come back home, but she refused. There was nothing more we could do, which was the last time I saw my cousin again. Sikh families would never allow their daughters to marry Muslim men. It was frowned upon back then.

Another cousin of mine had become pregnant out of wedlock and been disowned by her parents. This was a shock as both my sister and I were very close to her. She was a couple of years older than me, and our parents told us not to contact her again. My sister and I didn't listen, though, and would meet up with her secretly and spend time with the baby.

During this time, I heard many more stories of certain youngsters in our family and within our community running away from home or being kicked out for shaming the family. I would often hear my mum and aunties gossiping about it, and I would always think one day someone will be gossiping about your children if you keep gossiping as you do. I didn't like listening to these conversations. They terrified me and made me fearful of where these people had gone and how they would survive without their families.

Chapter 4

A Young Buck

Childhood is one of the most incredible times in a person's life. The innocence, sweetness, and compassion of children are unmatchable. Since I grew up in a close-knit family, I had a good childhood, and there was never a dull moment. We would always find activities to indulge ourselves in, and they were always enjoyable.

During this part of my life, I spent most of my weekends with my grandparents Maa Ji and Papa Ji. Maa Ji would tell me stories about when she was younger in Malaysia and how she would play with her sisters and brothers and climb trees to collect 'Durian,' a smelly fruit but which is really good for you. She told me how girls weren't allowed to go to school when she was young, and I always felt very sorry for her as I enjoyed school and couldn't imagine being told I couldn't go because I was a girl. I know Maa Ji missed Malaysia very much; she missed her family more than anything and the hot weather. She had learnt to speak Punjabi when she had married Papa Ji and cook Punjabi food as in Malaysia, her mother tongue was Tamil, and they ate other Malaysian cuisines. She would dress in salwar kameez, too, even though back home in Malaysia they wore a buju kurung, a knee-length, full-sleeved blouse and long skirt called a kain and in extreme heat sarongs tied above the chest. She tried very hard to fit in with the Punjabi culture, but she missed her own roots deep down.

I would notice this when Maa Ji would be on a call to Malaysia. She would speak Tamil, and my siblings and I would laugh and make fun of the way she was talking as it was completely different from Punjabi, and we did not understand one word of it. It sounded like she was just making words and sounds up. She would always spend the rest of the day crying and feeling sad after the call and say how much she missed her brothers and sisters. Papa Ji was also fluent in speaking Tamil. He had picked this up when he had lived there. My grandparents had never taught or spoke to their children in Tamil and only taught them Punjabi. Maa Ji said this was because the father's side of the family was the main mother tongue you teach your children. This was a shame because I would have loved to have spoken and understood Tamil. Maa Ji worked as a cleaner in the local hospital. Many other Indian women worked with her too, and they were all friends. We would often play with their grandchildren too when they came to visit.

Papa Ji was a very strict man. He would never let us dance or dress up in any appropriate attire. If he saw that my sister or my cousins or I had just our bare arms uncovered, he would order us to put a jumper on right away. When we danced, which we always did, he would charge at us to stop. I recall running around the house dancing deliberately to set him off. He would chase me and grab my long plait and sit me back down and say that *"Girls are not permitted to dance and that it is not what girls should do."*

Papa Ji told me that when he came to England in the 60s, he could not get a job because there was a lot of racism:

he wore a turban, and every job he went for, he was turned down and felt it was because of this. So, he took off his turban and found work, and provided for his young family at the time. He eventually got work in a factory making steel teapots. Papa Ji had dementia, and it was a struggle at times to watch him forget things and not know what he was doing or saying.

Maa Ji would sometimes take me to the Hindu temple known as a Mandir, and I enjoyed this as it was quite different from going to the Gurdwara. Firstly, I did not have to cover my head as I did in a Gurdwara. But I did anyway, as I just felt like it was more respectful. Secondly, there were lots of statues of different gods and goddesses, and they intrigued me. Nobody else ever went to the Mandir, just Maa Ji when she could. I would stay with them and watch old Indian movies like 'Amar, Akbar and Anthony,' a story of three brothers separated at birth and brought up in different religions. One was raised Christian, one raised a Muslim, and another a Hindu. I also remember watching 'Nagina,' a story about a snake that takes on a human form to avenge the killers of her snake husband. These two movies were my favourites.

Maa Ji made the best *roti* and curries. I learnt a lot of cooking skills just by watching her cook. Papa ji taught me how to use a knife to cut potatoes and onions. I would always help with the cooking. I felt safe and loved when I was with Maa Ji and Papa Ji. I knew they cared and loved me deeply. Visiting my grandparents is still one of my fondest memories, and I cherish them deeply.

We had a new addition to our family during this time. My mum had brought us a baby dwarf rabbit. He was grey and white in colour and the sweetest little rabbit. We named him 'Kulfy,' which means ice cream in Punjabi. At first, my dad was not happy about the rabbit, so his hutch was located outside in the garden. The first night he slept out there, we woke up to find his hutch door open and Kulfy shivering under the hutch in a little ball. We lived behind a train track, and foxes were common. We would often see them in our garden in the evening. My dad realised that a fox might have tried to eat him, but Kulfy managed to hide under the hutch, which was a small space, and a fox wouldn't have been able to reach him there. That was his first and last night outside. Dad also then formed a special bond with Kulfy, and it was almost like it was his rabbit now and not ours.

My dad is a very quiet man in general and quite reserved other than when he has had a drink; then, he will be more open to conversations. I don't know why but most of the men in my family are like this. They don't talk much and only say very little and never really give you eye contact and in particular to girls. My dad wasn't any different. He would say the bare minimum. Now that he was fond of Kulfy, all his attention when he came home from work would go to him. It was nice to see him interacting with the rabbit as if he was a baby. We didn't get any of that anymore as we were all growing up.

Kulfy was a big part of our family. He would sleep in the house, and we even trained him to poo only on newspaper in a certain place in the house. We even took him to visit relatives with us at weekends. They didn't mind; they knew how special he was to the family and, in particular, to my dad. We would take Kulfy to the park and even took him to Drayton Manor Theme Park with us, leaving him in the car and taking turns to watch him and let him out to play on the grass. My brother would say, *"Dad speaks to Kulfy more than he speaks to us."* My sister and I would just laugh it off but deep down, we knew what my brother was saying was true. Still, we couldn't say anything to my dad as we didn't want to upset him or think we were ungrateful: we had this invisible fear of my dad. Even though he never shouted at us or upset us in any way, we were just frightened of getting into trouble with him. His silence was enough to make us fearful of him. And at the same time, it took his attention off us, and we could get on with the things we were doing or shouldn't have been doing.

When I was fourteen, one of my aunties came over from India, and I was allowed to go back with her. This was my first ever holiday abroad. This was the first time I would be away all summer from my siblings. My dad didn't want to send us all, and as I was adamant I wanted to go, he let me with some persuasion from my aunty.

When I arrived in India, I remember how hot and muggy it was. There was a smell in the air too: not very nice. It was an eggy kind of smell that I had never smelt before. It was a smell that would come and go.

Despite that, I absolutely loved India. I stayed with my dad's family in our village. My dad's family consists of large members. I had four uncles whom I called Thaiya Ji and their children living in the house too. There was lots of living space, two kitchens, and plenty of space outdoors. Our family members were farmers in India, so we had acres of land and a separate house on the farm along with buffalos, billy goats, cows, and chickens. We had dogs who guarded the house and the farm too.

My cousins and sister-in-law lived in the house. I felt so free in India. I met many of my dad's family and learnt to speak Punjabi more fluently; I even started to learn how to read and write it. I also wore a salwar kameez all the time.

My cousins would take me to school with them on some occasions. I didn't really understand what was being taught; I just went so I could be with my cousins. The school they went to was nowhere near as nice as the school I attended back home. The classrooms were just dull and empty, with no displays, nothing, just empty walls and old seats and tables; some students even sat on the floor. There didn't seem to be any structure either; everyone just seemed to be doing whatever they wanted. We would cycle out of the village and into the main district through the hustle and bustle of India's traffic. My Thiaya Jis were quite strict and would have restrictions on where and which route we could go. I notice no one followed any rules here. You just drove, cycled, and walked wherever you could find space.

My cousins were a couple of years older than me, so we really got on well. I noticed that the girls and women in the house constantly had chores to do. I would join in, too, starting with 6 am wake-up calls to go to the farm and milk the cows. We also had workers who helped at the farm and with some house duties. They were treated like family and would eat with the family too. I loved how everyone in the village knew everyone and looked out for you as if we were one big family.

I never felt homesick during my summer in India; I felt like I was home, loved, and happy. My Thiaya Jis never said no to me. Anything I asked for, they would get for me. I treated them like my dad, and they treated me like their daughter. They reminded me so much of my dad and looked very much like him too. They had a lot of authority in the village, and I noticed how respected they all were by others.

My cousins and I would go to the funfair and have fun. We would jump on tempos and go shopping for bargains. I only ate *roti* and curries during my visit to India.

I visited many Sikh Temples and learnt a lot more about Sikh history. One of my favourite visits was to the Sri Harminder Sahib Ji, also famously known as the Golden Temple in Amritsar. I felt at peace here. I absolutely loved how in Sikhi, everyone is treated as equals and that no one is better than anyone else and that the door to a gurdwara is open to all from all points of a compass. However, I would wonder why the caste system was still in effect. It just didn't make any sense to me as to how we were all supposed to be equals while treating one another differently because of our job status and what family we were born into. The caste system divides Hindus and Sikhs into categories. It is an ancient practice that, in my opinion, just segregates people.

I noticed that there was a lot of poverty in India, and this saddened me. Every time I left the village to go anywhere, I would almost certainly encounter someone begging for money from me. I hated saying no it made me feel so bad, so I would then leave the house with pieces of fruit from some of our trees and offer them to the beggars; some took them, others were quite rude and said they only wanted money. I would sometimes get pushed and shoved and grabbed by beggars trying to take anything they could from me. My cousins would look out for me and say, *"They know you are not from here, and that's why they do it."* Once a lady tried to snatch my glasses off my face. I couldn't believe it; how could she even see in my prescribed glasses? When I shouted for her to leave me alone, I noticed her glasses were broken, and she had cello tape around them. This incident scared me, and I was quite shaken up, but afterwards, I felt very sad for her that she had to do that. If I could have given her my glasses, I would have, but neither of us would have been able to see properly!

I also experienced some perverted behaviour from outsiders when I was travelling on buses and tempos. Men would try to touch my legs or brush up against me. It was disturbing for me. Once I walked onto a bus that was very crammed. But, since there was an empty seat next to a man wearing a turban, I sat down beside him, thinking I would be safe. But he tried to touch my leg too, so I got up and swore at him in English. Everyone was looking at me like I was crazy, and no one said a word to him. He just sat there like he hadn't tried to touch me. I began to think, *"Now I know why this seat was empty."* I looked for my cousins who were standing behind others all jammed into tiny spaces, so I just waited to get off with them.

I would write letters to my family, tell them all about what I was up to and how I was missing everyone, and how we will go together next time, but I still wasn't ready to go back either as I loved being in India.

When it came to leaving and going back home, I

refused to leave. It took my dad many phone calls and conversations to get me back on a flight. Three weeks after my original flight, I decided I had no choice but to go home. The attendance officer at my school was on my parents' case about why I wasn't attending school and thought they might have shipped me off to India to get an arranged marriage. So, I thought before this actually does happen, I better get back home. But I would be back again, I promised myself.

My trip to India made me realise that I was fortunate to have the life I had compared to my cousins back in India. Soon as they finished school, they would have to get an arranged marriage, move out of the family home and take care of their husbands' household. I at least had the option of going to college and maybe even university. After this, I became more ambitious and wanted to do well in school and get good grades, so I started trying more in class. I still struggled with maths, though, but I was in the bottom sets and didn't have consistent teachers. I knew this was going to be my weakest subject. I focused more on my English lessons as I enjoyed writing and reading more at the time.

My dad already made us attend the local Punjabi classes after school, and at first, it was just a place for us to meet up with our cousins and mess around. I actually enjoyed it compared to my brother and sister. My brother would moan about going to lessons and say he didn't want to learn Punjabi and that it was boring. He would hide behind cars and skip lessons. On some occasions, my dad would catch him and send him back into class. Punjabi was one lesson I never missed or tried to get out of doing. I enjoyed it and tried hard because I wanted to actually learn how to write and read it. I was already writing weekly letters to my cousins in India and learning a lot. We were also taught some Sikh hymns too; which we were made to sing at the gurdwara. We were all so embarrassed when we did this, sitting on a stage in the gurdwara singing Sikh hymns we had been taught. We laughed and giggled through most of it and didn't take it seriously at all. I managed to take my GCSE in Punjabi during this time and achieved an A grade. My parents were really proud of me and even framed my certificate and hung it on the wall. This gave me the confidence to try hard and achieve good GCSE grades in my other subjects. I left school with eight GCSEs except for maths, which I had to re-take the following year at college. However, I was very proud of myself.

Chapter 5

College

At sixteen years old, I started the next part of my journey at Henley College, situated on Coventry's south side. It was only a twenty-minute bus ride from my house, and my brother was already attending college there. I enrolled in the Business Studies GNVQ course and A Level English course, along with having to retake my maths GCSE. At school, I had found business studies very interesting, and even though I wasn't sure at this point what I actually wanted to do in my career, I knew that it would have something to do with business. This was a two-year course, and by the time I would've gained my qualification, I would have had the opportunity to apply for a place at University. I knew by now that I wanted to go to university and study for a degree and choose a university away from home to be more independent. I definitely knew I didn't want to get married as my mother did at sixteen.

The college consisted of a wide range of ethnic backgrounds; you had Indians such as Sikhs, Hindus, Muslims, Bengalis, and many West Indian students. We were the majority in this college, and I found less discrimination or labelling there. Making friends was easy when I first started as I already knew some girls who already attended college, and they seemed to know everyone, so they were quick to introduce me.

My lessons were spaced out throughout the day, so I had plenty of free time. It was nothing like school, where you only had five minutes to get to your next class. There was plenty of opportunities to mingle with others. I made some good friends at college, some of whom still play a big part in my life now. My first year at college was just an opportunity for me to become a rebel. Soon after my first term at college, I started to follow the crowd and began drinking during the day. I had all sorts of drinks such as Bacardi, Bottles of Hooch, Smirnoff, Diamond white, 2020, Vodka, JD, and Southern Comfort. There was a smoking room in the college, and I would be surprised by how many Indian girls and boys smoked.

It was in my second year of college that I started smoking Embassy Number One cigarettes. Practically everyone I was hanging around with was smoking then. During the summer, my parents sent my brother and sister to India. I didn't get to go this time as I had already been. I was really upset that I didn't get to go and felt really lonely at home without my siblings. A friend of mine would come over to see me, and we would go for walks and just talk about life. She was having problems with her family and was quite unhappy and had started to smoke - she offered me a cigarette, and I decided to smoke with her. After that, I was always in the smoker's room at college and buying cigarettes along with alcohol. There were occasions when my mum smelt cigarettes on my clothes, and I would just say I had gone to my friend Michelle's house, and she had smoked. I would use that as an excuse for why my clothes smelt of cigarettes.

We would attend day timers, which were basically

parties held during the day instead of night. These bhangra day timers were set up mainly for the Indians as at that time, going clubbing was not allowed by most Indian parents. So, we would all get together, buy alcohol and jump onto buses and trains to go to these day timers. While they were mostly in London, Birmingham, some were in Coventry. We would get drunk and spend the day dancing to Bhangra, RnB, hip-hop.

My friends and I would plan the lies we would be telling our family about why we would be late back from college, mostly that we were going to the library after or to one another's houses. Once we had our stories straight, we would then come up with excuses to tell our teachers why we couldn't be in for lessons. Next, we would get whatever money we had and chip in for bottles of alcohol.

Most of the time, I was already drunk before I even got to the day timer. Once in, I would spend the whole time just dancing with friends. I absolutely loved it. There were times when fights broke out, too, but I never got involved. I would then go home and just stay out of the way from my parents. I was petrified if they smelt any alcohol or cigarettes on me, I would be caught. I always made sure I had plenty of chewing gum and perfume so I could hide the smell.

On one occasion, I attended a Valentine's day timer, and there were around twenty of us who got on the train to Birmingham. We were drinking alcohol and smoking cigarettes. Some of them were smoking weed too, and I decided to have some. We were so loud on the train and didn't care for other passengers. When we got to the place, I was so drunk I didn't even make it into the club. I was paralytic. It was my first ever experience of being so drunk. I vividly remember getting into an ambulance and then waking up in a hospital. I had a drip attached to my arm, and I felt awful. One of my friends, Zarah, had come with me to make sure I was ok. The rest had carried on enjoying their day and entering the Valentine gig.

When I came around, the first thing I said to her was, *"What time is it?"* I needed to get home before my parents got in from work. My friend was also now worried. She was going to get home late too. I had lost my jacket, and I was feeling very cold. I remember her giving me her jumper to wear. When the doctor came in, he asked me questions about what I had been drinking, but I said I couldn't remember. He asked my name, and I made a name up as I was scared my parents would be contacted - that would be the end of me. I was told they wanted to keep me in during the night. There was no way that was going to happen. We had to get on a train back to Coventry in forty-five minutes. I managed to have the drip taken out of my arm and told Zarah to get me a sandwich, as I was so hungry. She returned with a tuna sandwich. As soon as I ate, we walked out of the hospital and managed to get the next train back home. I was so grateful to Zarah for staying with me. She had never once said to me how her day had been ruined and how she hadn't got to go to the day timer and enjoy herself. She was just happy that I was okay. She hadn't drunk any alcohol or smoked as she was a Muslim, and it was against her religion.

I managed to get home a little later than usual, but my parents didn't suspect anything. I was off college for a week after this incident, recovering. When I did return to college, there were rumours that I had my stomach pumped, which of course, I hadn't. Stories like mine were common. I still carried on going to day-timers and getting drunk. I hadn't learnt any lesson from it at all. Other than that, I was a little embarrassed. I never ended up in a hospital again but would still get drunk. I did feel guilty about lying to my parents, but this guilt was mainly when I was at home. Once I was out and just having fun and feeling free, I would just try to forget about it for a while.

There were a lot of Muslim students at college, and I got on well with them. Their families were much stricter than the Sikh families, though. I would often see some of the girls get on the same bus as me wearing their hijabs, and soon as the bus had passed their houses, they would transform themselves. They would fold up their hijabs neatly and put them into their bags. They would take down their long hair, brush it and apply lipstick, mascara, eyeliner, and blusher. They would also change their clothes. Then they would light up a cigarette on the bus (we were allowed to smoke on buses at that time). I had no idea that the girls I saw at college all day actually didn't leave their houses like that until I witnessed it for myself. They knew if their parents saw them dressed the way they were, they would be in big trouble, so they did it in hiding. I felt grateful that I could wear and dress how I pleased and my parents wouldn't mind. I only wore a little bit of lipstick and occasionally eyeliner, and my mum was fine with this. When we got back on the bus to go home, they would wipe off all the makeup, change clothes and put their hijabs back on. They were almost unrecognisable. They would then spend their evenings going to the mosque.

I also had some really genuine male friends who would look out for me like I was their sister. If ever I needed a lift home or advice, they would be there to help, and vice versa; I would also give them advice about their girlfriends. I would hide from my brother around college, so he never saw me with any of them. I would be worried that he would tell my parents. It was easy to dodge my brother. He was doing his own thing with his friends, so we barely saw one another. I felt embarrassed of him, and he felt embarrassed of me. We were getting to an age now where it wasn't cool to be around each other, other than at home.

Some boys at college started to take an interest in me. Boys asked me out, and I would feel embarrassed and say no first; there wasn't anyone I particularly liked. But when we went to these day timers and got drunk, boys would try to take advantage, sometimes I would end up kissing one, and then the next thing I knew, word got out at college, and now we were dating. At that time, if you kissed a boy, that's it, he was your boyfriend, and you were his girlfriend, and obviously, all this happened in secret, nobody ever got an idea.

I did date some boys during my college years. They were all Indian, and I didn't date them for more than a couple of weeks or so. Most of the time, I would regret dancing or kissing them at the day timers, but I was drunk. I would spend my time hiding or running away from them whenever they wanted to meet up. I was not looking to be in a relationship at all. I enjoyed parties and getting drunk with friends, and these boys would always seem to try and hang out too much.

Many of us were dating in college and hiding our relationships from our families. We would gather in the canteen or the smoking room and discuss who was dating who and who had now split up with whom. We were a proper little community, gossiping just like our parents did. I would hear such and such has had an abortion, so many girls went through this. I would also support some of my friends who were now sexually active get through their abortions.

I had only been taught about sex at school. Indian families didn't talk about sex. Even when a kissing scene came on the telly, we would all get shy and try to start a conversation a few moments before, so we didn't have to endure the embarrassment of watching it. Our parents also never sat any of us down to talk with us about sex. It was no wonder when we became sexually active, we didn't have a clue. My mum didn't even talk to me about periods - I learnt that from school. And when I did start my period, I remember feeling embarrassed to talk to my mum about it. I told her I was bleeding, and I think I have started my period. She said, *"What? You can't have."* I was twelve, and I was confused and for a moment thought I hadn't, but I *was* bleeding. She then grabbed a sanitary pad and literally threw it at me, and I caught it like I was catching a ball. Nothing more was said on the matter. After this, she just brought extra pads, which I helped myself to.

Despite all my drinking, smoking, partying, and skipping lessons, I managed to do well and pass my courses. I would do most of my catching up and studying at home. I had more discipline at home. I had no choice but to study that way, and I had more time for fun at college.

Teenage years are those years when you think you are doing everything right and hardly pay attention to anyone's advice. You want to explore more in the world and meet new people. It was the same for me. When I was a teenager, I wanted to do everything on my own and wanted to live my life according to how I wanted. This is how I often got into arguments with my parents because they would disagree with me, but I was adamant about my decisions. I could not tell them about my adventures because I was sure I would get scolded for it, which I always wanted to avoid.

However, those were only the teenage years of our lives. We made reckless mistakes and learnt from them, and that's what matters the most. When a person learns from their mistakes, it shows that they have evolved.

Chapter 6

Relationships

At age seventeen, I started working in the city centre at a food court, making and serving pizzas. I would work every Saturday and Sunday. I felt so grown up having my job, and it gave me some more freedom. I also used the excuse of having to do extra shifts to meet up with friends afterwards. I would get paid weekly cash in hand, and by the time I had walked through town to get home, I would have already spent my wages mostly on clothes, hats, and bags.

It was my last year at college. When I had not long turned eighteen, I left my job and applied for another job with my sister at McDonald's. My sister also joined the same college later and went on the same path of partying, drinking, and dating. I wasn't a very good influence on her at this stage in our lives. If our parents ever found out that we were involved in these activities, they would feel disappointed and ashamed.

McDonald's paid much better than my last job, and I could get more shifts too. Quite a few people I knew from school or college worked at McDonald's, so it was a nice working community at the time. My work colleagues gave me the nickname 'Nin' here, and so I was also known by this name. My friend, Nathan, from school, even worked there, so it was lovely to see him and have jokes as we used to at school. I met Cassian here. Cassian was a British-born Jamaican West Indian. He was a little over two years older than me and had also gone to the same secondary school as me. But I didn't know him at school, just heard of him. He had said he remembered seeing me around the school. I was that chubby girl wearing long plaits. He said he didn't recognise me since I looked mature now. I was an average size 12, and my hair was never in plaits anymore; I would let my curls fly free. He also lived in Cheylesmore, about ten minutes' walk from where I lived.

My sister and I were assigned to taking orders at the till and payments or assigned to the drive-through. Cassian was one of the cooks in the kitchen. He had a good reputation and was liked by the managers. He worked very hard, and I could tell that he was a bit of a flirt too. Many of the girls who worked there liked him and would always be hovering around him, trying to get his attention.

Cassian got on well with my sister and me, and he could always make us laugh. He was probably the funniest man I had ever met. He would call me 'soniyeh,' which is the Punjabi word for 'pretty girl.' I would laugh and just smile back at him when he'd say this. He would tease me and say how I was the caramel ice cream and how he was the chocolate fudge ice cream. I found myself looking forward to coming into work and hoping he would be on the same shift. If anyone were rude to my sister or me, he would stand up to them.

My sister and I would try and work the late shifts, which were from 4 pm to12 am. This way, we could now attend clubs and pubs and forgot about the day timers; we had outgrown them. We would get picked up by our male friends, who we trusted and treated like brothers and who would always make sure we were dropped home safely. We were able to tell our parents that we were working late shifts, but of course, we were out with friends.

During this time, I had actually started dating a Punjabi boy from college. He wasn't even my type but was handsome. I was quite vocal and loud, and he was shy and quiet. When we were together, I would do all the talking. I only dated him for a few weeks, and during this time I was also starting to get feelings for Cassian. I found myself thinking of him often and couldn't wait to get to work to see him. Just the thought of him brought a smile to my face. I had never felt like that about anyone. We had a strong spark and were just drawn to each other. Cassian would call me at work when we were on different shifts, and I would feel a little uncomfortable because some of the girls would say, *"Why is he calling to speak to her?"* We weren't dating. And at the time, I would have been too scared to date a black man and get into trouble with my family. But I did, however, choose to flirt with him.

This went on for a few months where we were flirting

at work. Then one day, he turned up at college with his friends. They didn't even attend the same college as me, but here he was. I spent the afternoon hanging out with him and his friends. They were so different from how the Indian boys were. They made me laugh so much, and there was just this whole different demeanour about them, which I liked. I also felt safe with them.

Cassian had a flat near the college, and he invited me there one day. I had already told the Punjabi boy I had started to see that I no longer wanted to date him. He was fine about it. He agreed that we weren't compatible and should just remain friends. For the first time, I actually had feelings for someone.

I left college and walked over to his flat, knocked, and waited. I only had a pager at the time, and he had a mobile phone. I waited and waited and found myself burning up and feeling angry inside. About twenty minutes later, I started to walk back to college, feeling like an idiot for even saying yes to meeting him as this would have been the first time we met alone.

Once I got to college, he messaged me and said he was sorry he was late and that he was there now. I was relieved he hadn't forgotten about me, but I was still quite vexed because I had to wait for him, and I had never had to wait for a man before. Anyway, once I had spent a few moments thinking about it, I decided I would walk back there and see him.

When I got there, he said to me, *"Sorry black man's timing."* I didn't know what that meant at the time: all I knew was that he had made me wait outside and that had not felt good. He explained that he had to give his sister and mum a lift; when he said that, I was ok with it, and I understood.

I was amazed at how tidy and clean his flat was. You could see he took pride in it. He explained how the flat was his dad's and his and that they both had access to it. He made me a cup of tea, and we sat down and listened to music and talked. It was obvious we were both attracted to one another, so when he leaned forward to kiss me, I didn't hesitate at all.

I spent that whole summer falling in love with Cassian. We would meet at the flat and just kiss for hours.

We would just watch movies, listen to music and just laugh and have fun. Cassian would school me on hip hop and tell me about his favourite rappers; he loved hip hop music, and I would pay great attention too. We would get up and dance to the music. The time would just fly by. He already knew some Punjabi words, which he had learnt from his friends, and so I started to teach him more Punjabi and explain the meanings of the words. He would also listen to Indian music with me, and I would translate the meanings to him. He would write lyrics and rap to me, and I would sing Indian songs to him. He was so respectful and kind and never put any pressure on me to have sex. He would pick me up for work and drop me home. Sometimes he would drop me home on his bike. I didn't tell many people about our relationship other than my sister and some of my close friends. I loved every minute I spent with Cassian. I would get so excited meeting him, my heart would race, and I wouldn't want the time to end. We would hate saying goodbye to one another. The rest of the time, we would be on the phone with each other. I managed to get myself a mobile phone and would give Cassian a missed call. He would then call me back, and we would talk for hours. He wasn't bothered by how high his bill would be.

Cassian would write me poems and love letters. He was very talented. Everything always seemed to rhyme. I started writing back too. Every day before we said goodbye to one another, we would exchange our letters for us to read at home. Then after reading them, we would start writing the reply. On some occasions, Cassian and I would make one another's lunch for the day and meet up to exchange it. My lunch would always have a poem written by Cassian in it.

Cassian was familiar with the Punjabi culture. One of his closest friends was Punjabi. So, he knew that I would not be able to have a proper relationship with him. But the more we knew that being together would not be accepted by my family and community, the more we were drawn together. For the first time, I had actually met someone who I genuinely liked and had feelings for, and I couldn't be with him. Cassian would knock on my door with his friend and talk to me. I would panic, opening the door, hoping my parents didn't see. I was lucky not to get caught. My parents, by now, had accepted that my sister and I had male friends from college and work. They seemed to be ok with this as, at times when they had dropped us off, they had not minded.

Cassian was dark and handsome. He had the most amazing smile and an honest face. When he smiled and looked into my eyes and wrapped his arms around me, my heart would just melt. I loved the sound of his voice too. I started to love every bit about him and would still feel nervous around him in those early days. I had never felt like this with anyone. I had feelings I couldn't explain. He would always be trying to make me laugh and playing jokes on me. After six months of meeting up secretly, I felt so comfortable with him that I lost my virginity.

We were inseparable by now; any chance I got, he would pick me up from around the corner of my house. I would duck in the car so no one could see me. We would drive some distance so we could spend time together without getting caught by anyone. On one occasion, when we were going for a walk hand in hand, an elderly Indian lady walked past us and said to her husband in Punjabi, *"Look at that girl with that Kala." Kala* was the_Punjabi word for a black person. I didn't know this woman because I didn't recognise her, but she made me feel like I was doing something wrong. She gave me a look of disgust, and I ignored her and looked the other way. Maybe she didn't think I would understand what she had said; maybe she thought I didn't understand Punjabi. A part of me felt worried in case she knew my parents and told them, and another part of me felt some sort of anger towards her for saying that. I also didn't say anything to Cassian as I didn't want him to feel upset by it.

I started to feel guilty about what I was doing, and I would look at my parents and imagine if they knew what they would do or say to me. I knew deep down I could not have a relationship with Cassian and that I would need to stop seeing him because if I got caught, my life wouldn't be worth living. My parents didn't even let my brother's friends come over to the house when my sister and I were there. They were strict like that. If we were home, my brother would have to speak to his friends on the doorstep.

So, one day, I plucked up the courage to meet

Cassian and told him that we needed to stop seeing each other as there was no way we could ever have a relationship. We met at the flat, and as usual, he was full of life and trying to make me smile. He looked me in the eyes and told me that he had fallen in love with me. My eyes started to fill up with tears, and my heart started to pace. I wanted to tell him I felt the same and that I had fallen in love with him too, but I didn't. I told him we had to stop seeing one another and that this could not be carried on further. It pained me to say those words instead of the sweet reply he was expecting back.

His reaction was to walk out of the flat, and I could see he was upset. I was shocked. Instead of talking to me, he had walked off and left me standing there. I stood there for a moment and actually hated myself for upsetting him. I had only seen happy expressions from him till now. I felt anger within me that I had not meant those words but had no choice but to say them because I was Indian; I belonged to a different culture and had parents who would never accept this. I didn't care about what colour his skin was or what religion he was. To me, he was perfect in every way; he was perfect for me.

I ran after him, but he wasn't ready to talk to me at first. So, I grabbed hold of his hand and told him I was sorry and that I didn't mean what I had said, and that I was scared of my family and community. I told him how I really felt and that I loved him too and couldn't bear to be without him, how I missed him terribly when we had to say goodbye to one another, how I would be thinking of him day and night and how he made me feel when I was with him. He looked relieved I could see his expressions changing in an instant from sadness to relief. He told me he had been trying to find the right time to tell me about his feelings for a while now. We went back to the flat and spent that day just cuddling and being in one another's arms.

Cassian told me to close my eyes and imagine we were having a picnic in the park. So, I did. He then said, now imagine we have a son and daughter. So, I imagined a little boy and a little girl sitting on our laps. Then he said, now imagine your dad and mum joining us. And I did. This moment was so significant to me because I decided that I would have that life I just imagined. The only thing was that I wanted to do it the right way. I wouldn't run away or disobey my family. Instead, I would work harder and do everything in my power to make people see that the colour of someone's skin doesn't define who they are. Cassian was warm and loving, and I loved every part of him. I could not see my future without him.

After this, Cassian introduced me to his family, so I was known by the name Nin by his family members. When I first met his mum, he had to pop home and get something, so he invited me in. I walked in, and his mum was washing up. She said to me, *"You poor thing, you are friends with Cassian."* I just smiled at her and said, *"Yes, I know."*

Cassian lived with his mum, younger sister, and younger brother. I had never been to a West Indian family's home before, and it was a whole new experience for me. I knew no one would know my family, so I didn't feel worried about getting caught. One of the first things I noticed was the aromatic smell coming from the kitchen. I had never smelt food like that. I was used to smelling curry in the house and from outside in the street, even on my clothes, but this was a smell I didn't recognise. I was curious about what was cooking.

Cassian and his mum would ask me if I wanted to eat with them. I would say no at first as I didn't want to come across as greedy and felt embarrassed. I would look at what was on Cassian's plate and ask him questions. He would say, *"Here, taste it."* I would start by having a bite and then end up eating half his dinner. I was amazed at how the rice was cooked and how the chicken tasted; the food was so good.

Eventually, I started having my own dinner plate. I would eat ackee and saltfish (one of my favourites), yam, dumplings, green banana, plantain, rice and peas, curry mutton, jerk chicken, curry chicken, and soup. I hadn't just fallen in love with Cassian now. I had also fallen in love with Jamaican food. I found that the food was full of flavour, just like the curries I had been brought up with. The family would cook Jamaican food daily and have delicious Sunday roasts. My visits to Cassian's became more frequent now.

Cassian and I would spend time confiding in one

another about our families and lives growing up. We trusted each other completely and listened to one another intensively. His life growing up was very different from mine.

Cassian's parents separated when he was very young and had met new partners and had other children. I met Cassian's father at the flat for the first time. Cassian had given me the key to the flat and had asked me to let myself in as he was going to be late. So, I did, and then there was a knock at the door. I opened it, and a man was standing there, asking me where Cassian was. I said he would be here soon, and then he left.

I then started to light up a cigarette, and the doorbell rang again, and this time I opened the door with my cigarette in my hand, thinking it was Cassian, but it was the same man again. He looked at me and said, *"Tell Cassian to call me."* I said, *"Ok, who shall I say you are?"* He said, *"Tell him it's his dad."* My eyes widened, and I felt embarrassed. He looked so young and could have easily passed for Cassian's brother. When Cassian came, I told him his dad had seen me with a cigarette in my hand and that I was smoking in the flat. I may have gotten Cassian into trouble. He laughed about it and said it's cool. Yet if that was an Indian family or my family, no way would the response have been *that's cool*.

College was now coming to an end for me. I was nearing the final exams of my courses, and I had been given a conditional offer on the BA Honours Business Studies and Marketing degree at East London University. This would mean that I would be moving out of my home and finally being independent.

Cassian was always aware that this was my plan. He knew going to university was important to me. My brother chose not to go to university and started working instead, so I would be setting a milestone for our family. At the time, none of my cousins had gone to university, so I was the first.

Chapter 7

A Difficult Chapter

It had been eight months now since Cassian and I had fallen in love. One morning, I woke up feeling like I was going to be sick. It was quite a different feeling; I had never felt like that before. I spent most of my morning in the bathroom, wondering what was wrong, and then spent the next few days feeling nauseous and worried. My skin colour had changed, and I looked very pale. Whenever I looked at myself in the mirror, it felt like there was an entirely new person standing in front of it. I was waiting to get my period to get rid of my suspicions. But I had also missed my period and was now beginning to think that I could be pregnant.

I decided to go to the Well Woman's clinic in the town centre. I knew where it was because I had accompanied my friends there in the past. Panic filled my body. A part of me just knew that something was not right with my body and that I could be pregnant as I had never felt this way before. But I prayed that I wasn't, hoping that I just had some sort of viral infection.

Once I had done my urine sample, the wait seemed like forever. I was stopping my tears from rolling down my eyes. When the nurse told me that the result was positive, I couldn't hold my tears anymore. What had I done! I couldn't believe that I was pregnant. I had been careful, hadn't I? I asked myself all sorts of questions. I tried to pinpoint the moment this could have happened. My family flashed before my eyes and how they would know I was having a sexual relationship. I kept thinking how they'd have to face the shame that their daughter was pregnant and with a man who wasn't Indian and not even married to her. I felt ashamed of myself. My heartbeat started to become faster, and my anxiety levels were high. *"Breathe,"* said the nurse. *"It's ok."*

After I had calmed down, the nurse started to discuss my options. I jumped straight in and said, *"I can't have it. My family will kill me."* She seemed to know exactly what option I would be taking as she handed me a leaflet on terminating a pregnancy. The thought didn't even enter my mind about keeping it then. There was only one solution: abortion. I made a booking for my abortion that same day, and she picked a date that was two weeks later. I wanted it there and then, I thought. I hated feeling sick. I wanted to feel like myself again; waiting two weeks seemed like forever, but I had no choice.

I arranged to meet Cassian and knew that I needed to tell him. He was shocked too. I was crying and upset. He knew there would be no way that I could keep the baby. I told him I had already booked the abortion. He said that he would support whatever decision I made and that if I wanted to keep the baby, he would also be there for me and take care of us.

I had only shared this news with my sister. She was shocked but knew that I would be having an abortion; she didn't talk to me about it at all. She was busy living her college life like I used to.

I spent the next two weeks feeling sick but never

actually being sick. The only way I could get rid of the nausea was by eating. I found myself eating more and more throughout the day. This led to me putting on weight. Cassian would let me wear his jumpers. They were baggy, and I could hide my stomach, which was now starting to bloat. Smoking made me feel sick, too, so I stopped. I started to crave crisps and ice lollies: Cassian would deliver food to me secretly at my house, and if my parents were home, he would leave it on the doorstep for me to collect later.

I carried on going to college and spent my evenings in bed at home. At college, I would imagine telling my parents and them being happy for me. I would spend time daydreaming, thinking of a different outcome. Then I would go home, feeling confident that I had the courage to tell them, and then I would be able to keep my baby. I started to imagine what my baby would look like and found myself hugging my stomach. But as soon as I would see my parents' faces, I would be frightened of what they may say.

I started to feel very emotional and sad. I would find myself crying for the baby inside me that I was about to abort. I loved Cassian so much, and now I was getting rid of a part of us. I thought back to when he told me to imagine our future and our children. A future which I wanted and had decided I was going to work towards. Yet, here I was, getting rid of a baby; my baby, our baby. I felt like I had no choice at this time. If I had been given a choice, I would have done things differently. I imagined keeping the baby and leaving my parents' house to move in with Cassian and his family. I imagined myself pushing a pram and bumping into my parents and them ignoring me and not acknowledging my baby. I couldn't imagine hurting my parents like this. They didn't deserve this shame. They had shown and given me pure love when I was growing up, and I would repay them with shame and humiliation. It would also not have been fair to bring a child into a family who would not acknowledge them. That would hurt me more. For these reasons, I decided that there was no other option.

Cassian would spend time telling me I didn't have to have the abortion. He would support me. I would tell him I didn't have a choice and that I was sorry I had done this to him too. After all, he was the father, but I didn't ask him what he wanted. I just knew what had to be done.

I was attending day surgery, so I would be out that same day. Cassian drove me there and stayed with me. There were many girls in the waiting area, and I looked at them and thought they must all be feeling like I do. I smiled at them, and they smiled back. Some had come alone; others had their partners with them. I couldn't help but feel very sad for the ones who had come alone. There was no one to hold their hands. I felt blessed to have Cassian by my side.

I was put under general anaesthetic, and when I woke up after the operation, Cassian was sitting next to me, holding my hand. It took me a few moments to realise where I was, and seeing him gave me some comfort. My body hurt, and I felt the emptiness inside me immediately; I started to cry. I knew my baby was gone. I could feel the loss, and I could see it in Cassian's eyes too, he was sad. The moment was short-lived because now I had to get home before my parents got back from work.

A few days later, I woke up with blood all over my

bedsheets; my pelvic area was hurting, and the pain was unbearable. My sister helped clean up the sheets with me so our mum wouldn't see. I was experiencing blood clots. I called the doctor, who told me that there was a chance that the procedure had not been done properly. According to the doctor, some parts of the pregnancy had remained in my womb, which had resulted in blood clots. Apparently, 7 out of 100 abortions can carry this risk, and a second procedure is needed to remove the clots. An emergency appointment was made for me the following day.

The next day Cassian drove me back to the abortion clinic, a place I vowed never to come back to just a few days ago. By now, I was bleeding so much the blood was coming through my clothes. I was taken straight into the operating room. There was no time to put me to sleep, and the doctor removed the clots. I had never felt pain like this ever in my life. I lay there and concluded that I had deserved this pain for what I had done, that this was my punishment.

I thought I would feel back to my normal self after having my abortion. I thought everything would be as it once was. I thought Cassian and I could get back to laughing and joking with one another. But it didn't. Instead, I was depressed, in pain, sad, and even though I had my family and Cassian, I felt alone. By now, my friends had started to notice the signs of why I wasn't feeling well, and I was able to confide in them as they had had similar experiences. We felt one another's pain and were able to talk through our feelings and how life was unfair for us. We would cry and hug each other like we would at a funeral. We would discuss how we were restricted in the way we wanted to live our lives because of our culture. They helped me get through this sad time, knowing I wasn't alone.

I decided that this was not going to stop me from moving forward in my life. If anything, I would go to University, get a good job, and create the life I needed for when I was ready to have children with Cassian, so I could stand on my own two feet and not be afraid of how I would take care of my family. This experience made me more determined to succeed, and I would not let myself down ever again.

Chapter 8

University

I was excited to move to London and felt like there was finally something going on in my life. It seemed like time had stopped after the abortion. I could not even see the light at the end of the tunnel during that time. Cassian and I didn't talk much about the abortion but more about the future and how we would have a family of our own and get married one day. There were times when I felt like I wanted to talk about it, but I think Cassian felt like it would upset me if we did. However, I picked up all my broken pieces and got ready to go on a new adventure. The day had arrived where I would be leaving to go to university, and my dad and my mum's brother would be driving me to London. I said goodbye to my mum, who was crying and upset. I tried hard to keep my tears in because I didn't want to show my mum that I was upset too, but it was evident that I would miss my family.

When we drove off, I could see my mum staring out from the upstairs window at me.

The car journey was a little over two hours, and when I arrived at my halls of residence, I felt very nervous.

This was a new experience for me, and I couldn't explain to anybody how I felt. As soon as they had unpacked the car and moved all the boxes to my room, they were already through the door! They were in London, and they wanted to hit up the local pub for a drink. I would have loved for them to stay a little while longer, I tried everything I could to delay them, but they were gone. I ran after the car when it was time to say goodbye, tears streaming down my face and praying they'd turn back around.

I spent the afternoon unpacking, and by the evening, I had already met other students. Everyone was so friendly. There were many overseas students at the university too, so it was nice to make friends from other countries. It felt like a new kind of adventure. Cassian had driven down from Coventry that same evening and spent the weekend helping me unpack and settle in. We missed each other so much when we were apart. We were so deeply in love by now that the next three years of being at university were going to be a challenge.

My first year at university was quite similar to my first year at college. I was out all the time drinking and clubbing with my new friends. Some of my friends from Coventry would also come over, stay and go clubbing with me too. I would attend my seminars hungover and take my dictator phone to record what the professors were teaching. On one occasion, I even sent Cassian to my seminar with my dictator phone because I was so hungover that I couldn't attend it myself. I would spend days sleeping and nights out clubbing in Central London. If we were low on funds, we would just have drinking sessions and parties at the halls of residence. I would regularly contact my family at home and lie to my parents about how hard I was working. The truth is, I was rushing through the assignments and just barely passing.

Cassian and I would spend almost every weekend together, mostly at my place in London. He enjoyed the clubbing scene, too, and got on really well with some of the lads at the University. Cassian and I enjoyed dancing together. He would always keep an eye on me when we were out. He still worked at McDonald's during the week, and when we would part ways for the week, we continued writing one another love letters. I would have my wall filled with pictures of us and often take out my letters and read them repeatedly.

We enjoyed holding hands and walking freely in London. I didn't have to worry about anyone knowing me here and seeing me with Cassian and reporting back to my parents. We would often jump on the tube, go shopping in Oxford Street and go to nice restaurants. I lived on takeaways mostly, and the only exercise I was getting was dancing in clubs. I would miss my parent's cooking. I started to appreciate food more when I visited home. I missed eating *roti* with different curries. I would call up my parents before I returned and tell them what I wanted to eat. They always made me whatever I asked for.

There was a turning point for me that changed my

attitude about how I was behaving at University. A new club called 'Fabrics' had just opened in London, and my friends and I had decided that we would be going there on a Saturday night. Cassian was also staying with me that weekend. When we arrived at the club, I noticed how big it was. I was already a little tipsy from drinking beforehand with some friends, and I said to Cassian, *"If we get lost, meet me here."*

There was a big wall separating the dance floor and the bar. He didn't reply, but I knew he had heard me. Somehow, I got separated from the rest of the group, and while looking for them, I bumped into a girl I knew. She was happy to see me and was with a few guys I didn't recognise. She introduced me, and one of the guys asked me if I wanted a drink as he was going to the bar to get some for the others. I said yes.

I then remember a drink being handed to me and drinking it while dancing with my friend. After a short while, I started to feel really strange and confused. My legs started to feel like jelly, and I found it hard to move them. My head was spinning, and I felt nauseous. I started to look for

Cassian. I couldn't see him then I saw the wall I had said to him earlier to meet me at if we got lost and separated. I somehow managed to walk towards the wall, and Cassian was standing there. I fell into his arms. I was able to observe what was happening but completely unable to move. I remember two security guards carrying me upstairs, sitting me on a chair, and giving me orange juice, and then I threw up. I was crying and could not feel any of my body. I saw Cassian punching at the wall and wanting to go back downstairs, but the security men wouldn't let him. I blacked out this point.

I woke up the next morning feeling awful and back in my room. Cassian was sitting on a chair, arms folded, staring at me, and he had an angry look on his face. First, I started to think about what I had done and trying to remember, but my mind was blank. My head was sore, and my stomach ached. He asked me what I remembered, and I said not much other than I took a drink from some guy. He explained that someone had spiked my drink with a drug called Rohypnol, commonly used on date rape victims.

Cassian asked me how I could just take a drink from someone I didn't even know. I knew then I was in trouble and had done something really stupid, but I had innocently accepted the drink. I called my friend to make sure she was ok, and she was fine.

She said she had only met those guys that night and didn't really know them. Cassian was still angry about it. He asked me what if something had happened to me and how he would explain it to my parents. He gave me a big lecture on how irresponsible I was, how I wasn't taking care of myself, and how I should not be taking drinks off men I didn't even know. He was right. He drove me back to Coventry, and I spent the week recovering at home.

After this, I always made sure I never took a drink from anyone I didn't know, and I would buy bottled drinks too. I started to focus more on my studies and spent most of my weekends in Coventry. I would stay over at Cassian's, and we would often watch movies and spend time with his family.

Not long after, Cassian and I booked our first holiday

together in Alcúdia, Spain. I had lied to my parents and told them I was going with my university friends. They didn't question me further. I did feel nervous on the plane, wondering if anything ever happened to me. They would find out I was with Cassian and had been lying to them. These kinds of thoughts often popped into my head.

The weather in Spain was just beautiful, 30 degrees warm, and we had a lovely apartment. We didn't take sun cream as we thought we wouldn't need it. When I visited India, I never put it on, and it was very hot there. At the time, I thought only white people wore sun cream to get a tan, and we didn't need one.

We booked a boat ride, and I was burnt by the end of the day. My nose and shoulders were so sore; the pain was excruciating. Cassian was fine, though. His skin was tougher than mine. He helped me find a pharmacy and get some cream for relief. I was very moody because I had to spend the next day indoors. Cassian took care of me, and after this, I always made sure I wore sun cream. The heat in Spain was very different from the heat in India.

We rented bikes and would bike around the beach, eat and drink at restaurants and do lots of shopping. The people were friendly too. It was a memorable holiday. I felt so free in our relationship and didn't worry about anything. It was like all my worries were left behind in England, and we could just be us not having to look over our shoulder.

By now, all his family and friends knew we were a couple and accepted our relationship. No one ever made me feel like I was different in any way. Cassian would take me to family gatherings such as weddings, birthday parties, and christenings, and I would be fascinated by how the Jamaicans spoke Patois to one another. I would find it difficult at first to understand some of it, but I got good at lip-reading some of the words I didn't understand properly. I got to know his family well and felt like I was a part of it.

Cassian was my biggest supporter. He wanted me to do well and complete my degree. He would always tell me how clever I was and how I needed to stay focused and work hard. During my second year at University, I struggled to pay rent and buy food and books. I was living off my student loan and credit cards and working some shifts at a clothes store. I wasn't going out as much as before. I had moved in with some lovely girls who were working hard and shared the same interests as me.

I never asked my parents for help financially. I always told them I had enough money. They would ask if I needed anything, but I always said no. I didn't want to take anything from them in case they threw it in my face when I finally told them about Cassian. So, I decided I would quit university. I was going to tell my parents when I next visited them. I knew they would be disappointed, but I would manage to persuade them that getting a job would be better for me. I felt like earning money, and saving was what I needed to do.

I talked to Cassian about this, and he was adamant that I needed to complete my degree first. I was trying to convince him that this would be the best thing for me. After some persuasion from him, I decided I had no choice but to complete it. He said I was halfway through now, and I was clever enough to finish and get a better job after. He said I would be making a mistake if I quit so soon. He supported me and gave me money for food and books whenever I needed them. I carried on studying, and to this day, I am so grateful that he was there to help me when I was feeling like I couldn't see through my dream of having a degree.

I had lived in East London for three years now and managed to pass my driving test there too. Cassian and I were starting to talk more about the future now and how the time was getting closer to telling my parents about our relationship. We would discuss getting married in the future. Being around married people was something that I had grown up around, Cassian on the other hand, had not. His parents were never married, and they weren't married to their partners either, so it wasn't the norm for him. However, I still dreamt of our future wedding where all our families would be together to celebrate.

Chapter 9

Memorable Holidays

My relationship with Cassian was growing day by day. There was no doubt by now that we would be together forever. I had given him every reassurance that I would tell my parents shortly, and no matter what the outcome, I was his, and he was mine. He knew it was vital for me to have my family in my life.

I started this process by introducing him to my parents when he dropped me home one day. By now, my parents were fine with me knowing and having male friends. They accepted this, so I invited him into the house. When my parents came home, my dad shook his hand. This was a custom in our culture, males shaking hands to greet one another. I realised how crucial that introduction was. Now, when I was ready to tell them, my words would not be, *"I'm dating a black man."* They would be, *"I'm dating Cassian."*

This is what I envisioned. I didn't see the colour of his skin. He was just my Cassian and was beautiful in my eyes. Cassian would tease me and say he should turn up wearing a turban and pretend he was a Sikh, and then maybe my parents would be ok with it. We would laugh about it together, which made our situation not seem as bad as it was at the time.

My dad sat down and spent time having conversations with Cassian. The pattern of the conversation was similar to how my dad would greet any guest in the house. He asked how his family was and where he lived. My mum thanked him for dropping me home. I went into the kitchen to make tea. It was so nice to see this, my heart started to feel at ease a little, but I also felt upset that I was hiding our relationship from my parents.

Cassian told my dad he lived with his mum, brother, and sister, that his dad didn't live with him, and that he saw him every two weeks on the weekends when he was growing up. My dad looked sad and put his arm around Cassian and said, *"I'm sorry to hear this, but it's ok."* I loved that my dad was showing compassion towards Cassian. He was also trying his best to speak English with him too. He didn't stop long, and then when he got up to leave, my mum said, *"Thanks again for dropping Bubbly off. You are like a brother to her."* Cassian and I just exchanged glances at that statement. Finally, he said, *"No problem anytime."* Dad shook his hand again and said goodbye, and he left.

I called Cassian after to discuss what had been said, and once again, we laughed it off. Maybe mum had a feeling something was going on. He said he enjoyed meeting my parents and that they were nice people. And we didn't discuss my mum's comment ever again.

We started to plan and save for holidays whenever we could. We both loved to travel and especially together. Our next holiday was to Turkey, a beach resort in Kusadasi. I spent two weeks on the Atkins diet so I would look good in my bikini; I was a confident girl. I would always wear whatever I wanted and felt comfortable. Cassian would often tell me how beautiful I was, and he would just let me be me.

Turkey was amazing. Our days started off with

having breakfast together. I would sunbathe and get Cassian to apply sun cream on me. There was no chance I was getting burnt again. I would put it on him, too, but he thought it was pointless. He would say, *"I don't need sun cream. I'm black, and black people are used to the sun."*

I would disagree and put it on him anyway because if he did get burnt, I would have to take care of him and didn't want to jeopardize my holiday. It was a precaution. We would go swimming in the ocean and the swimming pool. I would love to read and take a book with me, and Cassian would wear his headphones to play some music. Then we would go to a nice restaurant in the evening, trying lots of different cuisines and afterwards, a club to end our night.

On one occasion, we went clubbing and climbed up onto the bar and started dancing, but nobody told us to get off. Everyone was just having fun. It was so much fun as we made friends with people from the hotel who were also from England and would go out with them. I would take pictures and put them straight into a photo album. I would think to myself, one day, we will show our children our pictures. There were so many beautiful Mosques, and I would love to hear when the call for prayer was made. This was my first experience of visiting a Mosque. The building was beautiful on the inside, too, with marble floors and beautiful patterns on the walls. And I felt at peace there.

Next, we visited the Greek island of Crete on this holiday. We spent more time relaxing and walking to different places on the island and sightseeing—lots of sunbathing and eating delicious cuisines and fresh fruit juices. Cassian would try to locate a pub that would be playing football matches. He loved football and supported Tottenham Hotspurs. His dad was a big supporter of the team, too, and Cassian had got his love for the team through his dad. He would often spend time at his dad's watching Tottenham play. I would try my hardest to be interested, and now and again, I would watch a match or two with him.

My dad was a big fan of football and supported Liverpool, so I grew up watching weekly matches on television. I supported Liverpool because I was a daddy's girl, but I would support Tottenham when I was with Cassian. This was to keep the peace. If Tottenham scored a goal, I would get kisses galore from Cassian. He would say, you're my good luck, and if they lost, his face was all screwed up, and his mood would be off for a short while, but it wouldn't take him long to be back to his usual happy self.

I was twenty-one years old now, and during this time, I also returned to India. One of my friends was getting married; she had agreed to an arranged marriage to a man in India. Her family had found her a suitable match. They had exchanged photographs, and the decision was made just like that. I had been invited as I got on well with her sisters too, so I took the opportunity to go back to India and see my dad's family. I missed them and thought about them often.

Now that I was older, India didn't feel like it did when I visited before. One of my cousins had an arranged marriage and lived in another village, and had a baby. It wasn't the same for me when I saw her, although I loved her dearly and was very happy to see her. I couldn't help wonder if I had been born in India, I would have had the same fate.

My other cousins had emigrated to America and Canada. My eldest Thiaya Ji's son, who I called 'Parji' (this is the Punjabi word for brother), his wife, whom I called 'Phabi Ji' (the Punjabi word for sister-in-law), and their young son now occupied the house. I was glad my Phabi Ji was there. I loved her. She was newly married the last time I had come to India, and when she moved in, she fitted in well with the family. I had the most respect for her; she was always up early doing her duties, and I never heard her complain once.

She would take me to visit her family, and they were so welcoming. I could see why she was the way she was. One of my Thiayas Ji's' still lived at the farm and carried out the day-to-day farming duties. I also spent time with my Poa Ji (my dads' sister). She was so loving and was always happy to see me. She would tell me how much she loved my dad and when he was little, she would always take care of him as a mother would to a son. He had not returned to India yet since he had moved to England to marry my mum. But he did keep in regular contact with them over the phone. I often wondered why he hadn't returned.

I was to spend five weeks in India. The first three were set to help make the wedding arrangements, and then the next two to do some sightseeing and visit family. This summer in India was a very hot one, and I forgot to take any sun cream. (Don't worry, I didn't get burnt). We went shopping for our wedding outfits, and my friend's mum was so kind she paid for anything I wanted. Her mum treated me like I was her daughter. I never felt like I was a friend; I felt like I was her daughter too.

I didn't eat much in India because I was experiencing diarrhea; everything I ate came straight back out, so my weight plummeted quite quickly. My friends and their mum would always keep an eye on me. I missed home, though and I missed being with Cassian. I would call him often and tell him how I was homesick and just wanted to come home. He would say, *"It's not for long. You will be back soon. Try and enjoy yourself, and if you really want to come back, then come."*

The wedding was great though we had so much fun together, we all loved to dance and would dance to our heart's content. Our outfits were beautiful, but due to the extreme heat, I couldn't wait to get out of my lehengas or saris. They felt uncomfortable. I would wear make-up and get myself dolled up like the others. My Parji once told me off about it. He said I shouldn't be wearing any makeup and didn't agree with some of the outfits I had picked out. I just chose to ignore him.

I ended my holiday in India after the wedding. I called my dad crying, saying how I was missing home and wanted to return asap. I told him how I couldn't eat much, and I was suffering from diarrhea. He was visiting his brothers in America at the time and had taken my sister with him. He told me to stop crying and that it would be ok. He would make plans for me to fly back home in the next few days.

Once on the aeroplane, I started to feel feverish, and my temperature was rising. We had to stop off at Akshabad in Turkmenistan halfway through the flight. The flight was full of Indians, and as I was sitting in the waiting area, I could see the bar, and only a few men were buying drinks from there and no women. I plucked up the courage to go to the bar and asked for a shot of whiskey. The barman and the men at the bar stared me up and down. By now, my nose was running, my eyes were red, and my hair was all over the place; I looked a mess. He poured me a shot, and I drank it in one go. It tasted horrible, but when I was young and feverish, my dad would get me a shot of his Famous Grouse Whiskey with a little honey in it and say, *"Drink this, you will feel better."* I did. I would sweat out the temperature. I felt so much better for the rest of the flight. People were staring at me; I didn't care.

When I arrived home, I saw the doctor straightaway. He checked me over and said I had an ulcer in my stomach. I would need to rest and start eating properly again and take medication to recover. I had to wait till I was better to see Cassian. It felt like the longest wait ever since I had to say goodbye to him when I left for India.

It took me a few days to feel like myself again, and the first thing I did was drive down to his house. I came running out of the car, and he came running out of his house.

We were so excited to see each other finally. He scooped me up in his arms, kissed me, and spun me around; our faces were full of joy. We had missed one another. He said I had lost weight, and my skin was darker as I had managed to get a tan whilst I was out there. I was excited to show him all the things I had brought for him and his family. I always did this when I went away alone I would buy souvenirs and gifts for his family and my own.

Not long after this, my cousin, who had emigrated to America from India, was getting an arranged marriage. My dad had decided he would be going and taking my sister and me along too. We were excited that we were going to Philadelphia in America. We got on well with our cousins. When we arrived, there were separate houses for the men and women. My dad would be staying a few streets away with the men and my sister and me with the women. We would get together during the day, but this was purely for sleeping arrangements. My dad was with his brothers and in his element. He would be drinking with his family members and enjoying the food, whilst my sister and I would chill with our cousins and their friends, helping ourselves with delicious food.

The wedding was colourful and fun, once again dressing up and dancing to the fullest. My cousin looked stunning, and her husband seemed like a nice person too. He got on well with everyone. There were times I would secretly sneak out to the phone box and call Cassian. My sister would cover for me. We did lots of sightseeing and visited New York and spent a lot of time shopping.

When we left America, I knew I would miss my cousins. We were all close; even though we lived thousands of miles away, we were close. On the flight back, my dad chose to sit in the middle of my sister and me, which was strange to me. He always chose to sit at the end of the aisle. He had had a few drinks on the flight, and I was trying to watch a film. He then nudged my shoulder and said in Punjabi, *"Bubbly, tu ve hunn vai vare soch?"* In English, it means, *"You need to start thinking of getting married now."* I felt sick; I couldn't believe he was having this conversation with me. My sister glanced at me and then turned the other way.

He had obviously had a few too many and was feeling courageous about saying this to me. He had never said anything to me before about marriage. He said if I had a boyfriend, I should tell him and that he was ok if they were not the same caste as us as long as he was Punjabi. He said to make sure he's not Muslim either. I wanted to end the conversation as quickly as I could and said, *"No, dad, there's no one,"* and *"Yeah, I'll think about it."* Cassian flashed before my eyes when I said this, and I felt bad. I could have used this as an opportunity to tell my dad, but I didn't. He was drunk by now, and I thought he would probably forget about the conversation. My sister and I then spent the rest of the flight trying to sober up my dad before we got home to mum.

My final trip during this time in my life was visiting my Massi Ji and her husband in Australia for three weeks. Cassian had decided he would drop me at the airport. We knew we would miss each other terribly. When it was time to say goodbye, he came as far as he could to the airport gate, and we hugged till the very last minute before I had to go. He had tears in his eyes, and so did I. I had taken some of the letters he had written to me in those early days to read on the flight and left him letters under his pillow for him to find when he got back home. I would often do this. I had bags of letters hidden at home.

My Massi Ji lived in Sydney now and had a happy and content life. Once again, I treated them like my parents, and they treated me like a daughter. They knew about Cassian and had said they would support me in any way they could when the time came to tell my parents. My Massi Ji was quite vocal to me about what I would have to face when the time came. I think she thought of her situation when she had to tell Maa Ji and Papa Ji about her white boyfriend. They were happy for me to call Cassian and speak anytime I wanted to.

I enjoyed Australia and experienced deep-sea diving at the Great Barrier Reef, shopping in Sydney, visiting the beaches and zoos, and sightseeing. My uncle was a manager in a marketing firm, and I had just completed my dissertation and was awaiting my result. He had suggested he could get me to work for a year on a visa in his marketing department; I was excited. Australia was a beautiful country there were lots to see and do. I said I would think about it.

When I arrived back to England, I mentioned to Cassian that I had an opportunity to work in Australia and I would stay with my Massi Ji. He could come and visit. Cassian told me straight. He said, *"If you go, then I won't be here when you get back."* I asked him if maybe I could go for six months, but he still said no, so I asked how about three months, and he still said no. Finally, he said, *"It's your decision but don't expect me to wait any longer."*

So that was that. I never thought about it again, and we never mentioned it again. Even I knew I wouldn't be able to stay away from him for that long.

It wasn't long after this that I arranged to meet my brother and tell him about my relationship with Cassian. I had already spoken to my sister, and we had agreed it was time to tell him and see if he would support me. I told Cassian that we would wait for my brother and sister to get married first because if I did it before, it might jeopardize their futures depending on the family they married into. I didn't want anyone to say to them, *"Your sister married a black man. We can't marry into your family."*

So, I thought I would go last, and it wouldn't be so bad. When I told my brother about me dating Cassian, his reply was, *"Oh phew, I thought you were going to say you're pregnant."* He took a big gulp, and my eyes started to fill; I explained and told him that I would get married last so that they wouldn't be affected so much. He agreed with me. He said he liked Cassian. He had met him a few times now and that he would support me when the time came. But we would at least need to let my parents know he was my boyfriend.

Chapter 10

Graduation

I successfully received my honours degree and was so proud of myself. My graduation was nearing, and I wanted so much for Cassian to see me at my graduation ceremony. After all, he had also played a big part in my journey at university. I also needed my family there too. This was going to be a proud moment. So, I decided that I would now tell my parents about us. I hoped and prayed every night that everything would be ok. I started by booking five graduation tickets. I even plotted a plan beforehand if my parents turned on me and beat me for the first time in my life; I was petrified.

My friends were aware of what I was going to do, and they would secretly come over and take my bags with all my things in and leave them at their houses in case I was told to leave the house suddenly, that way I could pick my stuff off them. I remember emptying my bedroom cupboards. My sister and I shared a room, and we took great pride in it. It looked empty now, and I took one last look.

It happened to be Diwali that day. I didn't even realize. I wasn't interested in celebrations much with my family anymore. I had managed to get out of attending a lot of weddings and functions using the excuse of university and work. My brother and sister would stand by my side. It was decided that they would tell my parents that they supported me and that they liked Cassian. He was a good person.

Cassian was sitting, waiting nervously at home. He and his mum had already told me that I was welcome to live with them if I needed to. But this made me feel uncomfortable; I couldn't move in down the road and bump into my parents. I actually didn't know where I was going to go, but I knew I was welcome there and would be taken care of.

When the moment came, we were all petrified and kept glancing back at each other, and my heart was racing. Dad was sitting down eating a big bowl of cereal, and mum was sitting next to him watching television. I had my car keys placed near the front door, just in case I needed to run out of the house.

I took a deep breath and said, *"Mum, Dad, I have something to tell you. I have a boyfriend, and it's Cassian."* It was like a scene from the Indian dramas that my parents used to watch. There was a long pause; silence filled the room, and everyone was still for a moment before a reaction was given. All eyes were on my dad. He got up calmly and walked out of the room upstairs to his bedroom.

Next, we looked at mum. She had a sunken look on her, and she walked into the kitchen. A few seconds later, we heard a cry, and when we walked into the kitchen, my mum was crouched on the floor, weeping, arms around her waist. The three of us just looked at each other, and I thought it was a bit overdramatic for my mum. I had never seen her cry like this. I was also afraid that she might come charging at me like a bull. We didn't know what to do, so we just stood there. She then got herself up and walked past us and went upstairs to my dad.

We waited for what seemed like an eternity, hardly saying anything to each other. I was still waiting for them to come down and tell me to get out of the house or at least slap me. Eventually, my mum came down and said, *"Your dad said everyone get up to bed."* Then she went upstairs, and their bedroom light was turned off.

That was it; no other reaction or communication at all. They didn't give me a chance to say anything. I had a whole speech prepared in my mind about how I would tell them I would wait and be the last to get married and how much of a good person Cassian was, and he would take care of me. My brother went up to his room and shut the door. My sister and I did the same. We were both crying in bed that night. I messaged Cassian what had happened and that I was ok that I would be in touch. My friends were also waiting on my call. I did the same and told them I was fine and would be in touch.

I didn't sleep that night; I don't think anyone did. My dad was due to do an early morning shift and at 6 am, he knocked on our bedroom door and said, *"Bubbly can you drop me to work?"* I jumped out of bed straight away and replied, *"Yes, dad."* His eyes were bloodshot, and I could tell he had been crying and not slept either. There was silence in the car. I had to drive him to Royal Leamington Spa, and that was a good twenty-minute journey. He didn't say a word to me other than when he got out of the car and told me to pick him up after work, and I said, *"Yes, dad."*

I was all over the place; I was so torn. I thought doing things this way would be the right and honest way to go about it, but I was hurting everyone around me. I happened to drive past the hospital that I had had my abortion in, and I pulled over, staring at the entrance. I sat there in my car, tears rolling down my face and crying out loud and for the first time wishing I hadn't even been born.

What was the point in having a life if you couldn't live it freely the way you wanted? I would think of Cassian and feel bad for him. What had he done wrong? He could have been a father by now. He wanted children. He would say, *"We will have a football team."* He had been waiting five years from when we met for me to tell my family. He didn't deserve this. He couldn't change what colour he was, no one could, or what family, community, or religion they had been born into. I would think of his family and how much I respected them; we were all the same in my eyes. I decided I couldn't make things the way I had dreamed and that society would never let me. I was sick of living this secret life.

It was still quite early, and the morning traffic hadn't yet built up. I drove to a bridge and started to build up the courage to jump. I sat in my car, debating with myself, first imagining what the impact would be if I just died. Who would miss me? Would anyone even cry for me? I thought if I died, then my parents wouldn't feel ashamed of me and that I would just be a distant memory to everyone.

I thought of Cassian and how he would be alone without me but how he was better off as he could find someone who didn't have to hide the relationship. I cried and got out of the car. I walked over to the bridge and looked down. The first thought that came to me was, what if I jump and don't die and just injure myself? How could I make sure

I was dead once I jump? So, I looked at the cars driving down and thought, *"Right, I will jump and hit a car. That way, the impact would be sure to kill me."* I wasn't bothered about the pain; I just wanted it to be done in an instant. Then I started to think of Maa Ji and how I knew she would miss me when she'd find out what I had done if I jumped.

I could imagine her crying uncontrollably. I couldn't do that to her. I started to think about how she and Papa Ji had somehow overcome their own obstacles and how they had successfully stayed together despite all this. Yes, they were both Indian but still from two different parts of the world and cultures. Cassian and I weren't any different. I thought of the person driving their car that morning and who would hit me, how they would feel afterwards, and the devastating impact it would have on them. I couldn't do that to a stranger. I now realised there was no way I could jump. I got back in the car and drove home.

Mum had gone to work by now, and I spent the day with my friends bringing all my stuff back home and putting it away. I couldn't eat and just felt sick all day. The time came to pick my dad up from work. When I picked him up, he had his hand bandaged up. I asked him what he had done and if he was ok. His eyes were red, and he said, *"I'm ok. I just had an accident at work."* I drove him home, and I felt so guilty. Was that my fault? Dad never had accidents at work, and today he had hurt his hand.

The atmosphere in the house for the next few weeks was difficult. No one talked to one another much, and we only had basic conversations with our parents, such as how many *rotis* you wanted to eat when it was dinner time. We would go to bed super early too. I would meet Cassian during the day and sit in his car crying. He was sad. They hadn't even acknowledged him. I would say to him that maybe he should just move on and let me go. It was never going to happen, but he was adamant he would wait till however long it took. My graduation ceremony was near, and I knew I couldn't take Cassian. How could he just turn up there? So, I threw his ticket in the bin; he understood.

On the day I got dressed and ready to go to London with the family. My brother and sister were ready, and as my mum was coming down the stairs I asked where dad was, and she said he's not coming. My heart sank, and tears filled my eyes. My brother looked at me and said, *"It's ok. We are all going with you."*

I had been waiting for this day in my mind. I had prepared for this day to be attended by my whole family and Cassian. That was going to be the start of my new life with him and my family on board. But now, that wasn't the case. We made the most of the day, and I collected my degree with a heavy heart.

Not long after, I met up with Cassian and gave him a picture of me in my graduation gown with my degree. He proudly thanked me and placed it in his room on the shelf. He was proud of me and told me that.

One day I was sitting on my bed, and my friend had come to see me. I would stay home more often now as I didn't want my parents asking me if I had met Cassian, and I would only have to lie again, and now that they knew, they would see through my lies. My mum came in and said to me, *"Why did you do this? You know it was never going to work.*

You come from two totally different cultures!"

My defenses flew up out of nowhere, and I had the courage to reply. I said, *"How do you know it isn't going to work, and so what if we come from different cultures?"* She stared at me, and I felt like I had been too brave speaking back to her. She then said, *"Look, don't see him for a year, and then we will talk about it."* I just said, *"Ok."* At that moment, I wanted her to just go away. I could see my friend felt uncomfortable too.

I told Cassian what my mum had said, and we decided she had said that so I would maybe forget about him. He was upset by this. I was now feeling angry at how my parents had just tried to brush this all under the carpet as if it had never happened.

We couldn't bear to be apart, so I hatched another plan which Cassian agreed with. I would find a job and move away to get my independence, and we would secretly move in together. I could keep coming to visit my family like I usually did, and we would wait till my brother and sister were married and then try again.

Chapter 11

Developments

My mindset was changing now, and I had managed to find a balance between working, seeing Cassian, and being around my family. It was almost like everything that had happened was now forgotten at home. My parents carried on as normal, and life at home continued.

I started working at HSBC Bank in Sheffield. It was a 6-month contract, and so I was able to move out of the family home. I would, however, come over often and stay at Cassian's. I would also be home to see my family when I could. We decided that we would buy a property in Coventry when I was back, and I would just continue telling my parents I was living in Sheffield. Hopefully, in time, they would come around once they realised how long we had been together and waiting patiently.

Cassian was later unable to buy with me because he was in the process of helping his parents out purchasing other properties at the time. I, therefore, managed to buy my flat in Coventry, which we both moved into and started to live together, sharing the bills and taking care of our home.

As a couple, we had matured together now. We had a good circle of friends and enjoyed nights out and evenings in together. Cassian would work late shifts now at a parcel company, and I would work during the day. The flat was a newly built property, so we spent time and consideration when decorating it. We would take it in turns to cook and kept our home tidy. His family would often visit us, and we would invite guests over for dinner as we liked to entertain.

Soon after, I left my job and started tutoring Maths and English to secondary school children at home. I enjoyed this job as it was flexible, and it gave me satisfaction knowing I was helping children in their studies. I know how difficult I had found certain subjects at school, so I felt I could relate to these children. I also spent this time teaching myself some maths I had never understood before, such as

Algebra. I became my own teacher, buying books and spending my free time studying and doing online courses. There was no surprise then when I decided I wanted to work in schools. I got myself a job in a local school as an Educational Assistant, and to my surprise, they needed a Punjabi-speaking person, so my GCSE Punjabi came in handy for me.

I enjoyed this job and found myself in the classroom with pupils who reminded me of my own friends back when I was at school. I could see the similarities in the struggles students faced. I wanted to be a good role model and do my best to support them.

Some of my friends were now married and having babies. Although I would be happy for them, I couldn't help but feel a little envious and wonder when I would finally get married and have my own family. Sometimes I would think maybe I never will because of my abortion at eighteen and that because of this, I didn't deserve to be a mum. At times I would find myself crying and so decided I would start writing diaries about the way I was feeling. I would often write when Cassian left for work before I went to sleep. (I still have these diaries).

During this time, Cassian and I visited Paris. I had booked this as a surprise for Cassian's birthday. I chose Paris because it was a romantic city and we were in love, and it was only right we should make this trip together. He was thrilled when I surprised him. We did lots of shopping at the Champs Elysees and ate lovely food. We visited the Eiffel Tower and were excited about going up to the top. We walked hand in hand, and as we got closer, we both started to realise that it didn't look safe enough for us to go up. What if we fell off the side? So, we stood there staring up at it, and both agreed that we were too afraid and said we would pretend and imagine we went up to the top and tell the family when they asked if we went on the Eiffel Tower that we did.

We did fall out for a short while on this trip. We had just gotten ready to go out for dinner, and when we were walking on the street, Cassian stood on dog poo. I was so amused that I couldn't stop laughing at him. His reaction was hilarious to me. Cassian loved his trainers. He always had the latest trainers and would wear them with certain clothing items. He took pride in his appearance and always matched his trainers with what he was wearing. He would religiously wash his laces and spend time cleaning his trainers. So, you can imagine his reaction. He didn't appreciate me laughing at him either. He walked off and left me whilst he went back to the hotel to clean his trainers. I had to run after him as I didn't want to be left alone on the street and it was getting dark. Once he had sorted his trainers out, I apologised for laughing at him. I was feeling bad for him by now. I wasn't surprised when he started laughing about it, too, after seeing the amusement and humour in it himself.

When we arrived back home from Paris, we went straight to his family home. His family was waiting for him to celebrate his birthday. I got on well with all of Cassian's family members. They were my family too, and I know I was treated like I was a part of the family. I would look forward to eating the Jamaican food his mum had made. She was an amazing cook. They would put up decorations and have music playing. The little children in the family would be happy playing and running around in and out of the garden. We would all gather together. It reminded me of when I was young and my family would come together. We didn't do this anymore, Maa Ji and Papa Ji had both passed away by that time, and I missed them terribly. My family life wasn't the same as it used to be. Kulfy, our little rabbit, had also passed away, and my dad's sister in India had passed away, so he was very quiet and upset.

My mum was also very upset about losing her parents so close together. My Massi Ji had emigrated to Australia, and I missed her company and words of wisdom. I did make sure that I kept in regular contact with her. My Mamma Ji's marriage had broken down, and I missed seeing my two young cousins too. Cassian's family was very loving and caring. I admired the way they were. By the end of the evening, everyone would be dancing to Reggae beats. I would feel a little uncomfortable at first. That's because, although I loved to dance and in front of Cassian (I didn't care how I danced), I was shy in front of his family. His mums' partner, who we called 'Pops,' would get up and say to me, *"Come on, I'll show you it's easy. Just pretend you're milking a cow,"* so I would get up, bend my legs a little, stick my bum out, and pretend to milk a cow.

Soon after Paris, I had started to get severe cramp-like pain on one side of my pelvis, I tried to ignore it and thought it would go away, but it only got worse. I would feel faint and could barely stand up straight. I was also bleeding quite heavily. Cassian was worried about me, so I went to the hospital only to be told I was pregnant and that they had suspicions I had an ectopic pregnancy. I had no idea what that was. An ectopic pregnancy is when the foetus does not grow in the womb rather, it gets stuck in the fallopian tube and starts to grow there. It can be life-threatening as the tube cannot support the growth of the foetus. When we were told this news, it came as a shock. I was scanned, and it was confirmed that the foetus was growing in my fallopian tube, and if they didn't operate to remove it, I would have internal bleeding, which could be life-threatening. I was operated on immediately, and the foetus was removed along with my fallopian tube, leaving me with a 50 percent chance of conceiving again. When I came around, the doctor visited me and showed me pictures of the damaged tube and the foetus. I cried and just tried to make sense of the picture but couldn't; my mind was all over the place.

We were both devastated by this. In the hours I had known I was pregnant, I prayed that the baby would be ok. I decided I would keep the baby no matter what this time. I had my own home, a good job, and Cassian by my side. My family would just have to accept it now, I thought. Terminating the pregnancy didn't even enter my mind. But it was not meant to be.

I found myself writing in my diaries a lot more than usual. Spouting words of hate for myself and what a bad person I must be to have to go through these experiences I was having, how I must deserve this. Cassian did his best to console me, but I always felt guilty towards him. Another chance of becoming a father had been snatched away from him. I also now felt that I would never become a mother with only a 50 percent chance, and even then, I was told I was more likely to have another ectopic pregnancy if I did get pregnant. Once again, I picked up my broken pieces and carried on.

Chapter 12

New Beginnings

I had now turned twenty-seven years old and decided I needed to focus on my career. I had changed schools and started working as a Teaching Assistant. It was here that I decided I would complete my teacher training in business studies. I was accepted into the course at Wolverhampton University, ready to start in the new academic year. This gave me time to save and prepare for the course.

An unexpected turn of events occurred during this time. My sister visited me often and shared with me that she had met an African man and was five months pregnant. She told me that she was going to keep the baby. Initially, I was in shock; I could tell that she had been afraid of telling me. She still lived at home with our parents, and it hadn't been that long since she found out herself. I couldn't help feeling like I had neglected her and not been around much for her. I felt I hadn't been there for her like a big sister should have.

After some discussion, it was decided that I would be the one to tell my brother and parents on her behalf. There was no way of sugar-coating this; it needed to be done. I met my brother first and told him the news. He was in shock and asked where my sister was. I told him that she was fine and staying with a friend. We decided that we would tell my mum as she was due back from work soon. When my mum arrived, she looked at us suspiciously. Firstly, I hadn't told her I would be home that day, and secondly, my brother and I did look nervous. She hadn't sat down yet and immediately asked us what was wrong?

I took a big deep breath and told her that our sister was pregnant. My mum's face was pale, and she had to sit down. She was in shock. She put both her hands over her face and shook her head. She asked where my sister was and if she was okay. I told her she was fine but scared of what might happen. She started to cry, and my brother went over and hugged my mum and told her it would be alright. Seeing my mum cry, I started to cry too.

After a few moments, my mum wiped her tears. She said, *"Your dad will be home soon. We will need to tell him."* When she said this, my brother and I glanced at each other. I can't remember which one of us said *"I need a drink,"* but my mum responded by saying, *"Let us go to the pub. You can have your drink, and we can discuss how we are going to tell your dad."*

We ended up at our local pub, 'The Open Arms.' It was a hot sunny day, so we sat outside in the beer garden. My brother and I started to open up to my mum about our life at home. We told her that no one communicates with us. We have always just been left to our own devices. I mentioned how our sister lived at home, and no one even noticed she was pregnant. My brother and I told our mum that whatever the outcome, she was our sister, and we would always be in her life and support her. Mum listened to us intensively, and I could see she felt sadness from what we were saying but also knew we were right.

Mum decided that she would go and speak to my dad and tell him. She told us to stay at the pub and wait for her call. As she left, she said, *"Wish me luck."* We gave her a big hug, and she left. My brother and I sat there silently for a while. I felt bad for my brother; he had always supported my sister and me. He was our big brother, and we had become distant over the years. I felt quite guilty that I hadn't made much of an effort to be with him or my parents. I used this opportunity to tell him that Cassian and I lived together in Coventry; there was no need anymore to keep my little act up. I felt relieved.

An hour or so later, mum called and said to come home. My brother and I took a very slow walk home. We were both petrified as we knew that dad now knew. We wondered if he would disown her, and if he did, we both agreed that we would tell him that we would always be in her life. When we arrived home, the house was completely silent. My dad was sitting in the same place as he was when I told him about Cassian a few years ago.

My mum was by his side. He had tears in his eyes. I started to cry and walked over to him and put my arms around him. He hugged me back. I couldn't remember the last time I hugged my dad. I said, *"We're sorry, dad."* After a few moments, he said, *"It's okay. Tell her to come home everything will be ok."*

I explained how she would be home in a few days and that I would let her know it would be ok to come home. Dad had asked about her boyfriend, and I had told him he was nice as I had met him a few times.

That evening the four of us spent time talking about the way things were and how no one had noticed any changes in my sister. My mum and dad listened to us, and my dad said that he was sorry. I could see he felt responsible for all that was happening. He asked me about Cassian, and I told him everything. I told him how much I loved him and how we just wanted to have their blessing.

My mum asked how long Cassian had been waiting, and I told her nine years. My dad said, *"It's ok. Tell him to come around to the house."* Dad said he had nothing against Cassian. He liked him. He was a good man, but how would he tell his brothers and his family that his daughters were not going to marry Punjabis? I had sympathy for my dad. This was one of the things I would worry about - the extended family's reaction and how my parents would get the brunt of it as they would have to face them and know that people would be gossiping about them.

At this moment, I realised just how much our parents loved us and wanted us to be happy. My family had now turned a new chapter, and my parents were seeing us as adults in our own right. For the first time in my life, I was able to be myself and not feel guilty. I had my parents' support, and that was all I needed. Now I knew what feeling free felt like and what unconditional love was.

Cassian was close to my sister, and they got on well. They would often come together and tease me. My sister would tell him funny stories about our childhood, and he would tell her funny stories about me. They had a good relationship. He spent time talking to her about her new relationship, and she would confide in him.

When he had first heard about my sister's pregnancy, he was a little distant at first and needed some time to reflect on things. I know that this was not what we had envisioned, but it was how it was, and we needed to move forward. He supported us and knew that we needed to tell our parents, and once again, he was waiting to see the outcome. So, when I told him what my dad had said, he was relieved. We hugged and kissed, and I felt like finally, I could breathe.

My mum's birthday was a couple of weeks later, so my dad booked an Indian restaurant and invited my sister's partner and Cassian along too. Cassian was nervous about coming, but I reassured him it would be ok and that my dad was looking forward to seeing him again. I recall him saying, *"You sure I am invited?"*

"Of course," I said, still not believing it myself. When he knocked on the door, my dad opened it. He shook his hand and greeted him with a smile.

That was a memorable evening. Everything felt as it should be, and my parents laughed and smiled. I could see that they were happy because we were all happy. We enjoyed the food and cut a special cake for my mum. She was surprised we had gotten a picture of her on her cake. My brother made a big effort too, and most of the conversations between the men were about football.

My sister gave birth to a little boy who she named Rijkaard (pronounced Rye Kaard). I was there when he was born; I was able to be there for my sister like a big sister should be. I was very proud of my sister. She was brave and got through the pain of her labour in no time at all. She was up and walking hours later. My parents were smitten with Rijkaard too. He was absolutely gorgeous. She got married a few months later when she visited Africa and was happy being a new mum.

My mum and dad would come over to visit Cassian and me and have dinner with us. They told me they were proud of me and that I had brought my property. Not long after, my dad flew out to India and told his family about my sister and me and that he was now a grandad. His family was shocked, but from what my dad told me, most of them said that times had changed now and the youngsters of today make their own decisions, and as parents, we can only support them. I know that this was a big thing for my dad to do, and I respected him even more for doing this. He was able to put his own feelings to one side for his daughters.

When he returned, he had said to the three of us, *"You all have a key to this house. This is your home, and you can keep the keys and come and go as you please, along with your partners and children. They are welcome here, and if anyone doesn't like it, then that's their problem."*

My dad started to talk to us more and even stopped drinking, I felt like I could open up to my parents now, and I enjoyed talking to them. My mum told me that when she had told my dad the news, she had said to him, *"I will go with whatever you decide as you are my husband and I am your wife before anything else, but I will tell you that I carried my children for nine months and I will not be able to live without them."* It was at this point my dad had made his decision.

A short while after, my dad announced that he and my mum would be leaving England to live in Malaysia. My dad had visited Malaysia with my mum when Maa Ji had passed away to carry out a Hindu ceremony with her family where her ashes were placed in the ocean. He had enjoyed his first visit and got along with my mum's family, who still lived there. He was struck particularly by the temperate weather and how Malaysia was more of a modern country compared to India. We were surprised at first, but we knew that dad had made up his mind, and we couldn't change that. He asked my brother and me to fly over to Malaysia and take care of his and mum's visa. He was suffering from a bad back and was having treatment. Therefore, he couldn't come with us. He had also taken early retirement now.

Malaysia is a Muslim country, and many Chinese people live there too. The Indian community is the minority. My brother and I spent three weeks in Malaysia sorting out documents and visas. First, we spent a week in the capital city of Kuala Lumpur, and then we travelled on a bus to a town called Raub located in Pahang to meet my mum's family. One of my uncles said when he first saw me, he thought I was Malaysian. When he noticed my brother next to me on the bus, he realised that we had come from England. Malaysia is so beautiful. I could see why Maa Ji missed it now. I felt close to her here. Maa Ji's family spoke Tamil and some English. They didn't speak Punjabi and only knew some words, so we communicated in English with them.

We further travelled to the village where I met Maa Ji's younger sister and older brother. Her sister was the spitting image of her. I felt like I was with Maa Ji again being around her. She actually knew Punjabi as Maa Ji had taught her when she visited, so it was nice having conversations with her. She would put her tiny hands on my head like Maa Ji used to and show her affection that way. We met our mum's cousins and their children. I felt like I fitted in as they had hair and eyes like mine. I could now see where I had inherited some of my features from. They were welcoming and took good care of us.

One thing I noticed is that they would only eat after we had started eating first. The food was delicious too – so many different cuisines. We spent a week with the family, and they took us sightseeing and to many Hindu and Chinese temples. One of my favourite places was visiting 'Batu Caves.' I would be intrigued by the 15 m statue of Hanuman, the Hindu deity and the monkey commander of the monkey army. There were real monkeys in the temple, and they surrounded us. We climbed 272 steep steps to reach the Temple Cave. I was amazed. The statue of Lord Murugan is an incredible piece that is 42.7 m tall. We took so many pictures that day. The weather was also warm since Malaysia is located near the equator and therefore is hot and humid.

The family was happy to hear that my parents would be coming to live there soon. After a week, we had to leave as we had to take care of business back in Kuala Lumpur to complete the paperwork. My brother and I made the most of the week to ourselves. We would go shopping and go to bars and restaurants. My uncle from Australia was also on a business trip to Kuala Lumpur, so we had arranged to meet up with him too. It was lovely to see him. We spent the evening jumping from bar to bar and just having fun. My brother and I were bonding again, and it felt great.

When we returned, we informed our parents that it would take some months for their visas to arrive as my mum was born in Malaysia, they had been granted permission, but they would just have to go through the process of waiting. In the meantime, my dad's back had gotten worse, and we would all take it in turns to care for him as he could barely move. Cassian also helped by taking my dad to his appointments.

Cassian and I had started talking about our future now, and my teacher training course was nearing. He had not long turned thirty and said he wanted to be a daddy. I wanted to be a mum too but was afraid of having another ectopic pregnancy. Throughout all that had happened, I had put it all to the back of my mind. We weren't bothered anymore about being married. We could do that anytime we wanted now; we both knew people who were not married and had children and were getting married later.

After some discussion, we agreed we would try for a baby. I gave up my place on the course and started working as a supply teacher teaching mathematics instead. I found I had more work teaching maths as it was a core subject, and when I was ready to complete my training, I would do so in maths. This also allowed me to work in many different schools and gain more experience.

Chapter 13

A Blessing

Two months after trying to conceive, we found out that I was pregnant. I wasn't feeling myself and felt nauseous frequently. My menstrual cycle was still all over the place since my ectopic pregnancy. I took a pregnancy test and waited patiently for the result with Cassian. We were both nervous, and when the blue line appeared, we just took a big deep breath, stared at one another for a moment, and just hugged and kissed. We were so happy yet afraid at the same time as we knew that there was a chance it could be another ectopic pregnancy. I still couldn't believe it. I ran out of the flat and drove to get a few more pregnancy tests. I felt like I needed to be sure by doing lots of tests. The feeling I got from seeing those blue lines was excitement and fear all mixed into one. I would burst into tears and prayed that my baby had made it to my womb.

A few days later, Cassian and I attended the hospital for an internal scan to check if the baby was in the womb or if it was another ectopic pregnancy. I remember feeling unwell as I hadn't slept much because of worrying. Cassian held my hand through it all and reassured me that everything would be alright this time. And he was right. The baby was in the womb, and I was eight weeks pregnant. I felt so blessed that we were both going to be parents. Now we just had to wait for the 12-week scan. When we got home, Cassian was so excited he lifted up my top and started taking pictures of my tummy and talking to the little life inside me. I told him there and then that it was a boy. He said, *"How do you know that? It could be a girl."* I said *"I just know it will be a boy,"* I told him to remember that I had said this to him. I had always felt that my firstborn would be a boy. We decided that we wouldn't find out the sex of the baby and would let it be a surprise.

Instead of writing in my diaries, I had now brought myself some baby books and started to read up on pregnancy and birth. We waited till our 12-week scan to share the news with everyone. I was a little afraid of telling my parents that we had decided on having a baby, but it was more important right now instead of getting married. Cassian actually ended up telling my mum as I just couldn't get the words out.

Both of our families were happy for us when we told them the news. Cassian's parents had known about the ectopic pregnancy and had been very supportive at the time, so when we told them, they were excited. Cassian's dad was so excited, he picked me up one day and took me out with Cassian's sister to buy things for the baby. He said, *"Get whatever you want."* I was a little shy as I was worried about not wanting to spend too much of his money, but he reassured me that money was not a problem. This baby would be his first grandchild, so he was excited about becoming a grandad.

Afterwards, he treated us to dinner; it was a memorable day and one that I cherish. Throughout my first trimester, I continued to work as a supply teacher but was experiencing nausea, and I hated feeling like that all day long. The only time nausea went away was when I was

155

asleep—eating made it better slightly. I was starting to show now, and my clothes wouldn't fit me. I started to put on weight quite quickly, causing my back to hurt. I was four months pregnant now and one day whilst teaching a maths lesson I fainted. The children were requested to leave the classroom while first aid came to help me. I attended the hospital, and the baby's heartbeat was checked, which, to my relief, was okay. I had blood tests as I felt faint every time I stood up.

Cassian was by my side, too, while we were waiting for the results. I was then informed by the doctor that I had contracted the CMV virus and that I also needed to do a screening test for Down's Syndrome. The CMV virus is the Cytomegalovirus that can pass from the mother to the baby and cause complications. I was kept in hospital for a few days and was given medication. The test for Downs Syndrome is called an Amniocentesis, where you have to have a fine needle passed through the tummy into the uterus to collect a sample of fluid. There is a risk of miscarriage from this procedure currently 1 out of 100 women. Cassian and I discussed what we would do. We both agreed that the procedure was too much of a risk and that we were both prepared to love and care for our baby regardless of any disabilities. I was sent home with medication and told to rest and that I would need to be scanned every week. I had to leave work at this point.

Two weeks later, I got a call from the nurse, who informed me that I needed to stop taking the medication as they had mixed my blood test results with another patient. I did not have the CMV virus. Naturally, I was pleased, but I was also very annoyed that the hospital had made such a mistake. I wondered what the medication I shouldn't have been taking could have already done to my baby. The nurse reassured me that the medication wouldn't have affected the baby.

For these reasons, my pregnancy was a worry for both of us. I spent a lot of time crying when I was at home with Cassian. I tried my best not to worry, but it wasn't easy to do. I would feel my baby kicking and moving around inside me and hoped that everything would be fine. It wasn't until the final trimester that I started feeling better and preparing for the birth. Cassian attended every appointment with me. He attended the birthing classes too. We were excited and had prepared for the baby. I was in labour at home for 16 hours before Cassian drove me to the hospital. He was doing his best to support me, but I couldn't help but feel annoyed at him. I just wanted the pain to go away. When we got to the hospital, we were put into a room, and I was given a small container to do a urine sample.

I did my urine sample and then took off all my clothes and lay on the bed. Cassian said, *"The nurse asked you to do a urine sample, not take your clothes off."* I said, *"I don't care. I'm too hot, and I just want to take my clothes off and get this baby out now."* When the nurse returned, she said, *"Oh, I only asked for a urine sample, love."* I told her to check my cervix. When she did, she said, *"Oh, your 6 cm dilated. The baby is on its way."* I knew it; I could feel it. I only had gas and air after this point, and I was in a lot of pain. The nurse wheeled me to a room and said she would be back. I felt uncomfortable in the chair, and I saw a brown bean bag in the corner of the room and thought if I sit on that, that may be more comfortable for me, Cassian helped me walk over to it, and as I sat down on it, the bean bag popped right under me and just shrunk to half the size it was.

Cassian found this amusing and stated that it was now the size of a sultana! I gave birth to a beautiful healthy little boy weighing 7 pounds and 12 ounces. We named him Jeevan, which is the Punjabi name for 'life.' Cassian cut his umbilical cord and was full of joy. The first person he called to give the good news to was his dad. I had lost a lot of blood and had also been told that my womb had blood clots inside, which needed to be removed immediately. The procedure was done there and then by a doctor. I was in a lot of pain and, at the same time, full of joy at being blessed with such a beautiful baby.

When Jeevan was placed onto my chest, I looked down at him and thought, was he the same little boy inside me a few minutes ago? I couldn't believe I had become a mother now. He had stolen my heart in an instant.

I had planned to breastfeed, but Jeevan didn't take to

breastfeeding, and my back was so bad by now that I could barely walk. I cried a lot after the birth because the pain was unbearable. Cassian was a great dad to Jeevan and a supportive partner to me. During the first few weeks, he took care of Jeevan and me. I was so grateful he never complained and just got on with it. During this time, he was my rock. I started to have physiotherapy and acupuncture on my back and was able to do a lot more within a few weeks. I was enjoying being a mum and taking care of my household. It was what I had always wanted, and finally, I felt so happy. Jeevan didn't sleep well during the night, so we both lacked a lot of sleep, and often, this would mean we were both extremely tired during the day.

On one occasion, I hadn't slept for days. I accidentally thought I had put Jeevan's milk bottles in the microwave for five minutes to be sanitized. It turned out there was a *roti* in the microwave, and it blew up the microwave and caused a little fire. Luckily Cassian was there and put it out, but the whole flat was full of smoke. Cassian wasn't impressed and sent Jeevan and me to my mums for the night as he was worried the fumes would harm Jeevan.

Both of our families would help out and come and visit the three of us regularly, and we enjoyed taking Jeevan to visit family. This was also the first time since Cassian was a young boy himself he had sat in the same room as his parents when they would come and visit Jeevan with their partners. I remember the happy look on his face and how he would tell me he felt happy seeing everyone get along. Everyone loved Jeevan. He was a happy baby and very curious. Three months after Jeevan was born, my sister gave birth to a beautiful little girl called Khula. This is an African name and means 'to grow.' My sister would bring Khula over to play for the day while Rijkaard was at nursery. Khula and Jeevan would play together and even had their naps together.

Becoming a mother was something I had been waiting for a very long time. I felt joyful, elated, and empowered. I was now responsible for caring for a life, and Jeevan was dependent on me. I wanted to be the best mother I could possibly be to him.

161

Chapter 14

Life with a Baby

Jeevan was a summer baby, so we would spend most of our days taking him out to the park and watching him learn and grow. Cassian would work early shifts now in a new job as a delivery driver, then come home and help me take care of Jeevan. We had decided that I would not go back to work for a year and just enjoy being a new mum. I knew that this time was precious, and I wanted to spend as much time with Jeevan as I could. I would now write in Jeevan's baby books and write a daily log of all the things he was beginning to do, along with pictures.

We managed to get ourselves into a routine, and the days would just fly by. Jeevan was a happy baby and was very attached to Cassian. As soon as Cassian would walk in from work, Jeevan would get excited and want to be picked up by him. If Cassian left to go out, Jeevan would cry and not want him to leave, and Cassian would then take him with him. I would say he was definitely a daddy's boy. The flat was now starting to feel small to us as Jeevan's toys had now taken up most of the extra space we did have. Therefore, we decided we would try and sell the flat and look to buy a house.

Cassian's mums' partner 'Pops' was going to leave England to finish building his house in Jamaica during this house hunting process. He had been building his house in Jamaica for several years now, taking barrels back and forth with items to put and use in his house and spending months out there at a time. That meant that she would now be living alone as Cassian's other siblings had also moved out now and had their own families. She suggested that we all come and live with her at least for a year to save more money and then buy our house.

After some discussion, we both agreed that it would be a good idea, we spent most of our weekends at his mum's anyway, which also meant I wasn't far from my parent's house. So, it was decided we would move back to

Cheylesmore. A month later, we managed to rent out the flat and moved in with Cassian's mum. My family would often visit us, and I would frequently meet up with my sister and her children. Jeevan was crawling and talking now and was beginning to be very boisterous.

Whenever the front door would open, he would cry to go outside. He enjoyed being outside and playing. Jeevan started walking on his first birthday. We had hired a venue to celebrate his first special birthday and invited all our family and friends. It was a memorable day, and Cassian and I had put a lot of effort into organising it so that we could make it special for everyone. Our family and friends also made a big effort to help us with the food and decorations. My friend Michelle was the DJ for the party too, and she did a great job. We took so many pictures and videos that day, and everyone enjoyed themselves. Jeevan was passed around the whole day from person to person, and he was happy all his family were around him to celebrate.

Two months after, Cassian and I decided we would visit Jamaica. Neither of us had been there before. Cassian's grandparents and other family members lived there, so we thought it would be nice for them to meet Jeevan. I was looking forward to meeting more family members too. Pops had also now finished building his house and had invited us to stay with him. So, we left England for three weeks with our baby Jeevan on board.

Our flight was tiring as Jeevan struggled to settle, which meant he was in our arms for most of it. We had to keep taking it in turns to hold him. He always seemed to prefer it when Cassian was holding him, though. This meant that Cassian was tired a lot. When we reached Kingston Airport, I could feel the humidity straightaway. It was hot. We collected our luggage and then went through customs to show our passports. The security lady who was checking our passports asked me what my relationship with Cassian was. I felt a little offended by this, so I replied by saying, I am his partner and the baby's mum with a little attitude. She then pointed with her lips, shook her head to the right, looked me up and down, glanced at Cassian, and said *"Gwaan tru"* in a strong Jamaican accent. At this point, Cassian was dealing with Jeevan and holding some luggage, and we glanced at one another and sighed, then walked towards the exit where we could see Pops waiting eagerly for us. In the car, we both concluded she had asked because my surname was not the same as Cassian and Jeevan's and that maybe she thought that Cassian should be with someone of his own culture.

It was lovely to see Pops, and he was amazed at how much Jeevan had grown since the last time he had seen him. Pops had driven us to his house in Mandeville, located in South Central Jamaica. Pops' house was beautiful. He had built a house from scratch on land that he had purchased. The house was huge. There were at least five bedrooms, some with ensuite bathrooms. The living room was very spacious, and there was plenty of land around the house where many fruits and vegetables were grown. The garden was beautiful full of lovely bright flowers and fruit trees. The weather was amazing. I absolutely loved the weather when it was hot and enjoyed sitting in the sun.

Cassian and I did get bit by mosquitoes as soon as we arrived in Jamaica, and that was annoying, but it couldn't be helped. I was just pleased they had not bitten Jeevan. Pops also had two dogs guarding his house, and Jeevan loved playing with the dogs. We had taken a little blow-up swimming pool for Jeevan to play in and keep himself cool, and he loved spending time there. Pops' daughter Ramona was also staying over for a while, so it was nice to have some female company. We got on really well, and she adored Jeevan. Jeevan became very fond of her, too, calling her 'Aunty Mona' and asking her to pick him up all the time. Ramona would braid my hair for me and tell me how she wished she had my hair. She would say to me in her strong Jamaican accent, *"Mi waan tuh tek aff yuh ed a chop aff yeh eir."* I would laugh at her and say, *"What's wrong with the rest of my body?"* And she would reply by saying, *"Nah yuh too slim."* I wasn't actually; I had only lost some weight after giving birth to Jeevan and was struggling to lose the excess weight. However, when I visited Jamaica, my confidence grew as I noticed how confident the women were there. Jamaican women love their curves and dress to flatter their curves. In Jamaica, some Jamaicans view thinness as a sign of being unhealthy.

167

Ramona and I would often go out on our own and go shopping and get our nails done. I couldn't remember the last time I had days like this since becoming a mum. All my attention and time had been filled up doing my duties as a housewife and mum. Although we weren't married on paper, it didn't mean I didn't feel like I wasn't Cassian's wife. Cassian and I would often sit up on the balcony and enjoy a drink with each other. We would drink rum and coke. The rum had a natural sweet taste to it which I liked. I wasn't much of a drinker like I used to be but would occasionally have a drink if I felt like it. He could still make me laugh and poke fun at me, especially when I didn't understand when someone spoke to me in patois. I would ask him to translate. I found that my lip-reading skills weren't working so well in Jamaica as the Jamaicans spoke fast. He would say to me, *"Now you know how I feel when you and your family are all speaking in Punjabi."*

The food was just delicious. Every day we would have a big breakfast ready for us at the dining table. Sometimes I would eat cornmeal porridge and, on other occasions, fried dumplings, eggs, beans, and cornbread. I never ate this much in the morning back in England, but I was on holiday, so I was going to indulge fully, I told myself. Ramona and Pops also loved eating *roti*, and I would make *roti* frequently with our meals. Ramona and I even decided that we would open up our own food shop in Jamaica one day, and I would make the *rotis*, and Ramona would cook the fillings. It seemed like a great plan at the time. The jerk chicken in Jamaica was one of my favourites. Every time we went past this food stall called 'Murray's, I would make Pops stop the car and get me some jerk chicken. It would be wrapped up in foil, and I would carefully place it on my lap, eat it throughout my journey, and refuse to share it with Cassian. I would say to him, *"You should have got some for yourself."*

I would sit in the car and really enjoy the scenery and watching the Jamaicans going about their daily lives. I would be fascinated by the Rasta men and their dreadlocks. I loved listening to reggae music playing during the day and night. I could feel the love everywhere I went. We visited Cassian's

169

grandparents, who lived in Clarendon, just over an hour's drive away. They were so welcoming and treated us with so much love and respect. Cassian's grandmother had been preparing food all day for our visit, and she had made my favourite ackee and saltfish, yam, dumplings, callaloo, chicken stew, rice, and peas. The food was delicious. She was an amazing cook, and I felt like my stomach was going to burst by the end of the day. They had mango trees in their garden, and Jeevan would run over and pull the mangoes off. We took lots of pictures that day. We sat outside on the veranda, and Cassian's grandmother showed me pictures of their family. I could recognise some family members from the pictures who lived in England. I really enjoyed visiting Cassian's family, and I felt happy that his grandparents had met their great-grandson too.

Next, we visited Cassian's Mum's family, who lived in Negril. Negril is a town in western Jamaica and is known for its miles of sandy white beaches. We met Cassian's uncle and his family, and they were all so welcoming. I remember this day being a very hot one. I struggled to walk around in the heat and kept having to drink lots of water to stay hydrated and make sure Jeevan was well hydrated. They took us all to spend the day at Seven Mile Beach, which wasn't too far from where they lived. The sea was crystal clear, and the soft white sand stretched as far as the eye could see. It was just beautiful. Jeevan had his first experience of swimming in the sea here. Cassian carefully held his tiny hands and lifted him up into the sea, letting him kick his feet around and splash the seawater.

Jeevan was curious and happy. I took many pictures of them both and felt so grateful that we had this moment together. Visiting Negril was definitely a highlight of my holiday. I found Negril to be such a beautiful place with beautiful views and lovely people. We also visited Dunns River Falls and Park in Ocho Rios. The views of the waterfalls were just breath-taking. In between days of sightseeing, we would also go and visit friends of the family. So, it was nice to break down trips and meet up with people who had left England and come back to settle in Jamaica. Everyone was so welcoming and made a big effort with us.

I noticed how similar the Jamaican culture was to the Indian culture. The first thing they would do is fill you up with food and just want to make their guests happy. I have so many fond memories of my holiday in Jamaica and can say that from all the places I had visited throughout my travels, Jamaica would definitely be at the top of my list. Up until now, Malaysia had been at the top of that list. The views on the island reminded me of the views in Malaysia. The heat was also similar to the heat in Malaysia. I felt happy being around family and felt content in my life. When I left, I promised to keep in touch with Ramona too and told her when she comes to England to visit, she must come and stay with us.

When we arrived back in England, Cassian and I decided that we would try for another baby. We thought it was time now to give Jeevan a little sister or brother. I also mentioned that I would rather get my baby-bearing days out of the way and then focus on losing weight. Cassian never mentioned my weight issues to me, but he knew that I wasn't enjoying carrying the extra pounds. My back would suffer due to this most days. I knew it was because I was bigger in size. My physiotherapist had mentioned this to me. She said that because I had put a lot of weight on quite rapidly, my back would suffer. Jeevan also started attending nursery now, and I started to go back to teaching maths as a supply teacher. There was plenty of work in schools, and I could complete my teacher training in the future.

Chapter 15

Shanae

Two months after we had come back from our holiday to Jamaica, I found out I was pregnant again. Naturally, we were both so happy but knew that I would need a scan to check that it was not an ectopic pregnancy. We were much more relaxed this time around and not worried as we were when Jeevan was conceived. The scan showed that the pregnancy was in the womb and that everything was going well. I had decided that after my last pregnancy, I was not going to worry about anything this time.

I was going to keep a positive mindset throughout it all. We decided to wait for the 12-week scan until we told the family, who were all very happy for us. We also decided we wouldn't find out the sex of the baby. Cassian said it would be a girl this time, and he would get her a different dress for every day of the week. I was convinced that maybe we would have another boy. Jeevan was very active at this stage and getting quite a handful, and I could just envision him playing with a little brother.

I managed to go to work throughout most of this pregnancy and didn't feel so nauseous. I seemed to have a lot more energy this time around. I was also not as big as I was when I carried Jeevan, so I could manage more day-to-day tasks like doing the weekly shopping and hoovering. When I was pregnant with Jeevan, I was never allowed to hoover or clean the bath. Cassian would never let me do anything. He was very protective of the baby and me.

My dad had now recovered from his back problems, and the plans for moving to Malaysia were nearing. My parents had booked their flights for after I gave birth as they wanted to see their next grandchild. At six months pregnant, I slipped down the stairs one morning. I had just woken up and somehow tripped over my pyjama bottoms. Cassian and I went straight to the hospital as we were worried the baby might be hurt. After the fall, I was in a little pain and couldn't feel the baby kicking like I usually did. I was scanned, and the baby's heartbeat was checked. Thankfully everything was how it should be. On our journey home, we decided to go for a drive and parked up to have a chat. Cassian and I had a conversation about staying at his mums for the foreseeable future. I told him how I wanted to go back to the flat and just let it be the four of us when the baby arrived. Cassian agreed with me and said, as long as we were together, that's all that mattered. The year at his mum's had been a very busy one for me. The time had flown by, and I had felt like I just couldn't be myself there at times. Although his family was very loving and caring, I just felt like we were all just stepping on one another's toes at times. I wasn't used to living with in-laws and what I had envisioned felt very different from the real experience. I felt like I didn't get much quality time with Cassian like I did when he would get back from work at the flat. Instead, he would always be busy doing things for people.

At eight months pregnant, we moved back into the flat and prepared for our new arrival. Cassian would go out more now and leave Jeevan and me at the flat. He would always make sure we weren't left alone and call my sister or my mum to come over and spend time with me. Sometimes before he left, he would soak my feet in warm soapy water and give them a massage as my feet were quite swollen now. He would say he was meeting up with friends. I didn't mind so much; I trusted him and just wanted him to be happy. He would mention friends I didn't know from his new workplace, but I thought it was great that he enjoyed his job and made new friends.

I went into labour a week after my due date. This time around, I was in labour for eight hours. Jeevan stayed with my parents, and we had told him that the baby was on its way. He would just touch my belly and say, *"Baby coming, mummy."* I only had gas and air to get through the contractions. Cassian was by my side and gave me so much support. I gave birth to a healthy baby girl weighing 8 pounds and 5 ounces. She was placed straight onto my chest, and just like when I had first seen Jeevan, I fell in love with her tiny little face. She had entered the world sucking her thumb, and it was so adorable to see. She was absolutely beautiful, and I felt blessed to be her mum. Now that we had had a girl, I thought to myself, *"That's it. Now I have a son and daughter and won't need to be having any more babies."* Cassian cut her umbilical cord and said, *"I told you we would have a girl,"* and as before, I had lost a lot of blood and had blood clots removed from my womb by the doctor. I recall this time the pain was unbearable, and I was crying so much. The only comfort I got was having Cassian hold my hand. I stared into his eyes and prayed that everything would be ok.

A few hours later, Cassian collected Jeevan from my parents to take him to the hospital to meet his new baby sister. When Cassian arrived, he was pleased to hear that I had managed to breastfeed this time. *"Awesome,"* he said, *"We can save on baby milk now."* Jeevan was more interested in the biscuits that were on my table when he got there and, after eating a few, saw his sister for the first time. He stared down at her feet and said, *"Err dirty feet, mummy."* I told him that they weren't dirty and that because she had been in my tummy for so long, they were a little wrinkly. Cassian and I found this amusing, and he had also managed to capture this moment on camera. After a few hugs and photos, Cassian left with Jeevan and came back to pick us up.

Both of our families were pleased to hear that we had had a little girl and came over to visit her with gifts. A week later, we named our baby girl Shanae which means 'God is gracious,' and Jeevan also turned two a few days after her birth. I thought that this was great both our children's birthdays would now be celebrated together just like mine, and my brother's when I was growing up. It took me two weeks to get used to breastfeeding. The pain of breastfeeding at first was worse than giving birth. It was excruciating. I had never felt physical pain like this. I almost gave up on a few occasions. Cassian would run out and get me cream and medication, and I would be in such a bad mood when I knew it was time to feed Shanae. I would start preparing for the next feed after she had fed on one breast. I would cry whilst feeding her and would just want to scream. My friends would come over and help me with the cleaning and daily chores on some occasions. They knew I was in a lot of pain, and I was very grateful for their support even though they, at times, would have to deal with my moodiness. One day, I woke up and fed Shanae, and the pain was gone just like that. I had a whole different feeling running through my body. A feeling of relief overcame me. I called Cassian, who was at work, and my friends to tell them the good news.

Shanae was such a good baby. She ate well and slept well too. She was an observer, just like Jeevan was when he was born. The only time she took her thumb out of her mouth was when she was being fed. She would spend most of her time in her cot watching Jeevan playing. When she'd be upset, Cassian couldn't console her, she was attached to me, and every time I left the flat to pop out to the shop, he would have to call me and say come back. As soon as I would return, she would stop crying. Cassian would take Jeevan out a lot more while I took care of Shanae at the weekends. I had a special bond with Shanae as she was reliant on me from breastfeeding. I did my best to take care of our babies and take care of the household. I had turned thirty whilst I was pregnant with Shanae, and I was content in my life. I was finally living my dream from when I turned eighteen years old and had first met Cassian. Life had given me my family and Cassian. I had been blessed with two beautiful little beings, yet once upon a time, I didn't think I would ever become a mother. I had wonderful friends in my life who supported me and cared for me. I had my own home and a career that I could make progression in. I felt grateful that by making my own decisions and following my heart, I had the strength to get to this point in my life. I felt that this was my destiny. I was one of the lucky ones who were able to live the life I had chosen for myself.

Chapter 16

The Dream

Two months after Shanae was born, we were preparing to move out of the flat again and rent a house in Cheylesmore. We needed more space. A few days before we moved our stuff into our new home, Cassian asked me if he could meet up with some friends. Over the past few weeks, he would come in after work, rush any tasks he needed to do at home, get ready and go out and not return till late at night. There were times I had prepared dinner for him, and he would say he had already eaten. I noticed how he took care of his appearance, too, spending more time in the bathroom and getting himself ready. I was barely managing to have a 5-minute shower every day, and every cup of tea I made for myself would be cold by the time I drank it.

That night he didn't come home. I remember having this uneasy feeling as he wasn't answering his phone, and then after a while, the phone was switched off. I didn't sleep all night and prayed that he was okay and that nothing bad had happened to him. Eventually, he came home later the following morning. I was so upset with him but relieved that he was okay. He had told me that he had had a few too many beers and so had ended up staying at his mum's. I told him he could have at least messaged me as he would know I would be worried. He had never done this before. He apologised and said it wouldn't happen again. We then went to stay at my parent's house for a couple of days before the property was ready for us to move into. Cassian had asked me if he could go and meet up with some work friends that night. I was a little annoyed and recall saying, *"You are always going out these days and just leaving me alone with the babies, and that's not fair."*

"I know. I'm sorry, and after tonight, I won't go out and will help out more, I promise," he replied.

"Ok, and don't be home late like last time and end up at your mum's."

He told me he would message me when he was

returning home, so I didn't need to worry. I told him not to disturb us when he came in and to sleep in the spare room as he might wake the babies.

I was exhausted that night and fell asleep right away. I woke up in a sweat. I had dreamt that I was sitting at a table making a jigsaw puzzle. I was pleased with myself as I had nearly completed it, and when I reached for the final piece, there wasn't one. Instead, there was a black penis on the table. I started to panic because it wouldn't fit when I picked it up to place it into the puzzle. Then I woke up.

I got up and walked to the spare room, and saw Cassian sleeping. I shut the door and carried on with my morning routine. But my dream was playing on my mind. When Cassian was up and dressed, I asked him how his night was, and he said it was fine and that he came home after a few beers. I then looked right into his eyes and told him about my dream. Whenever I had a strange little dream, we would talk about it and what we thought its meaning was. Cassian would usually say, *"You have some crazy dreams,"* but he would listen and be interested in what it could mean.

This time he said, *"Oh ok, I have to go to the shops. Do you need anything?"*

I said no, and he left. I stood still for a few moments and thought to myself, now that reaction was stranger than my dream. We had moved into the property now, and I was happy with the routine I had with the babies. Jeevan would go to nursery during the day, and I would take care of Shanae and do the daily housework and cooking. Cassian would go to work. Cassian had also started helping me a lot more with daily chores and even sent me a text message from work, saying how he knows he has been a little distant, but moving and going to work had made him stressed. He said he loved the babies and me and would start making more of an effort with us.

I recall reading that and feeling relieved and happy that I had this support from him, and the distance I was feeling from him would now change. I replied how it was ok and that I understood and how much I loved him and that things would be better now that we had moved. We had only been in the house a week or so, and Cassian had planned a day off. Jeevan was at nursery, and we had decided to take Shanae out for a few hours. I recall being in the living room, and Cassian played some music, and the two of us were dancing together. It had felt like we hadn't danced for so long with each other. He then picked up Shanae, rapped some lyrics to her and jiggled her around, and she would smile back at him. He then went upstairs to shave while I fed Shanae.

While I was feeding Shanae, Cassian's phone bleeped. I put her down in her bouncer and walked over to the cabinet where the stereo was as he had left it there. I picked up his phone and saw a message from a name I didn't recognise. I opened the message and read, *"Hi, how are you doing and when can I see you? I miss our cosy chats in bed!"*

My whole body started to shake, and my heart started beating faster. I felt rage all over me. It was as if my body was on fire. I quickly grabbed a pen, wrote down the name and number, and then threw the paper into a drawer. I ran upstairs, pushed the bathroom door open, and saw Cassian shaving and singing in the mirror.

"Who is Sha?" I asked with his phone in my hand. He turned to look at me, and I could see the shocked look on his face. His mouth opened wide, and he said, *"No one."*

When he said that, I slapped him hard on his face and repeated the words from the text I had just seen. He tried to reach for his phone, so I ran down the stairs in a panic. He kept asking for his phone, and I was refusing to give it to him. He then tried to grab it from me, and I shoved it down my jeans. Our voices were louder now, and Shanae had started to cry. Cassian picked her up and tried to console her. I was shouting and swearing at him to tell me who she was and whether he had been seeing someone else. He was just interested in getting hold of his phone. He then grabbed me and fought me for his phone. I tried my best not to give it to him, but Shanae was still in his arms, and I could see her swaying all over the place. So, I let him have the phone and took her off him. He was enraged and didn't care that her head was swinging in all different directions at the time. He just wanted his phone. That's when I knew. He then put his jacket on and left the house.

I took Shanae upstairs and put her in her cot, and she fell asleep. I sat on my bed next to her and started to cry. My body was still shaking, and I was in shock. How could he have done this to me? How could he have done this to our children? I felt sick and sat there crying into my hands. The dream I had now made sense to me. That dream was playing on my mind since that day, and how he had rushed off, so we couldn't talk about it. I thought about my family and how I had let them down. I thought about my children and what life they would have now. I thought about his family and how disappointed they would be. I thought about myself and what life I would have now. I felt trapped, scared, and afraid. I didn't want this life anymore.

Shanae woke up and started to cry. She was due another feed. I didn't hear her at first. It was only when her cry changed and grew louder I knew she was hungry. I stayed still on the bed, turned my head and stared at her, and watched her cry. Tears were flowing down my face, and it was almost like I was waiting for someone to come and pick me up and tell me that everything would be ok. Moments passed by, and by now, Shanae was crying so much I didn't recognise her cry. She had never cried more than a few minutes for a feed. That was when I realised that I could help her and stop her tears in an instant, yet mine would keep flowing, and no one was going to come and help me. I reached into her cot and picked her up, and fed her.

Silence filled the room. I looked at her tiny face and watched her feed, knowing that she was okay now. I told her I was sorry for letting her cry so long, and I would never let her cry for her milk again. I put her back in her cot, and she fell back to sleep. Cassian walked in straight after he had been gone over an hour now. I walked downstairs, and he had a look on his face that I had never seen before.

He looked angry. He took his jacket off, placed it on a chair, and then sat down on the sofa. I asked him where he had been, to which he replied he had gone for a walk. I asked him to tell me if he was seeing someone else, and he denied it. I asked to check his phone, which he gave me, and when I checked, the message had been deleted. I asked him why he had deleted the message, and he ignored my question. I started to ask more questions, all of which he ignored. I was crying and felt hopeless. He wasn't answering any of my questions. I bent down to my knees and begged him at his feet to please just tell me, and that I won't be angry, we can sort it out. He turned his head the other way and wouldn't look at me. I said to him, if you don't tell me today, things will never be the same again between us, you have a choice, and you have to make that choice right now. He then shrugged his feet away from my hands and didn't say a word.

When I stood back up, I turned and looked at his jacket. I picked up his jacket and smelt it. I could smell cigarettes from his jacket. I had not smoked in years, and Cassian never smoked. *"Does she smoke?"* I shouted at him and asked. He got up and grabbed his jacket. *"Don't be silly. I can't smell cigarettes. You're acting crazy."*

Over the next few weeks, Cassian would do his best to reassure me that nothing was going on and that I had imagined it. I started to think that maybe I was wrong and hadn't read the message properly. I had always trusted Cassian and had never thought he would cheat on me. He knew how I felt about cheating. I had told him throughout our relationship if he ever cheated on me, I would leave him, and if he was ever violent with me, I would leave. One evening he planned for us to watch a movie after we put the children to bed and cooked dinner. I was trying my hardest to forget about what had happened, and he was affectionate. It was when we became intimate everything changed for me. I realised that this was not my Cassian anymore. This man was an imposter.

The next day, I left the house and brought myself a bottle of wine and a packet of Embassy Number One cigarettes. I sat in the garden drinking and smoking. When Cassian came in, he asked me what I thought I was doing. I told him to leave me alone and that I could do whatever I wanted to, and that he didn't own me. He left me alone and went inside to take care of the children.

A few days later, I visited his mum and asked her if he had stayed at hers a few weeks ago. She wouldn't speak at first, so I had to repeat myself. Then she looked down at the ground and said, *"Yes, he did."* She was nodding her head up and down. My eyes filled up; I knew she had just lied for him. I turned around and left.

For the next few weeks, when the children were sleeping, I would spend my evenings drinking and smoking and lashing out at him and saying some hurtful things to him so he could feel guilty and tell me the truth. Eventually, he told me that he had only held hands with a girl at work. He told me her name was Charlotte and that he would never see her again and that she had left work. I asked him if she was a white girl or a black girl? He told me she was a white girl. I was full of rage and felt jealous – a feeling I had never experienced before.

Every time I looked at him, I felt disgusted with him. I knew he was insulting my intelligence. I could see the guilt in his behaviour. I was hurting. I would leave the house at night and drive around the streets crying. I didn't want to be in the same room as him, let alone sleep next to him. He never asked me where I was going. He knew he couldn't get me back as by now I had turned into someone else I didn't recognise. I would lash out, punch and slap him almost every day now and tell him how disgusting he was to me and how I would never let him near me again. I hated myself for hitting him; I just couldn't control my anger, especially when I knew he was lying to me. He would say to me, *"Let's have another baby and forget about what had happened."* I couldn't believe what he was saying to me. If I had known he was like this, I would never have had children with him. After that, I refused to have him sleep in the same room as me, and he would now sleep with Jeevan in his room.

At first, Cassian would take every slap, push and punch I gave him. Until one evening, he didn't come home again. I was calling him, and his phone went straight to voicemail. By now, I was barely eating and sleeping and had lost a lot of weight. My blood was boiling, and I felt that he was with her. I was so angry and upset I had washed and ironed his work clothes that day as he had to go to work the next day. I picked up the scissors and cut up his work trousers and felt some satisfaction. He arrived around midnight. I had already thrown his cut-up trousers outside the front door. He was fuming when he saw this, and as he tried to enter the house, I tried to push the door shut so he couldn't come in.

I was shouting and swearing at him to leave. He managed to overpower me, and when he pushed the door open, he grabbed me by my throat, dragged me to the living room, and threw me to the ground. I was in shock and struggling to breathe. He started saying sorry to me instantly, and he tried to put his arms around me, but I pushed him away and told him to leave me alone. I searched for my inhaler and took a few puffs. I was shaking and crying. All those weeks, I had been hitting him and wanted a reaction. I finally got one. He was bigger and stronger than me. I knew that and would wonder why he wasn't defending himself. But now, I knew that if I did continue to keep lashing out, he would. I was afraid of what the future would hold for our family and us now.

A few days later, when I was tidying up, I found the paper I had written her name and number on. I had totally forgotten about that. I managed to get his phone and checked to see if he had communicated with her. I couldn't see any messages, but I did see her number in his recent calls list. Cassian caught me with the phone and asked me what I was doing. I started shouting at him how he had said he wouldn't contact her again and that I had her number. He looked shocked and angry at me. He then told me that he had kissed her, and that was it. At this point, I was pacing up and down the room and shaking. I then asked him to kiss me how he kissed her. He looked shocked at this request, but he came over and pecked me on my lips.

"Now do it again," I said.

"No."

"Do it again," I repeated myself. Then he came closer to me and kissed me on my lips. I slapped him hard on his face and said that was different from the first time. Another fight broke out between us, and this time I felt afraid he might hurt me, but I carried on and on, winding him up, and eventually, he punched the wall. I ran out of the house with his phone and drove off in my car.

I parked up and sat in the car, knowing he couldn't leave the house this time as our babies were there. My hands were shaking. I then rang her number, and she answered, saying, *"Hi, who's this? Please leave a message."* She was giggling while she said this, and I put the phone down. To hear her voice made everything even more real now. I sat and cried for a while until I knew I needed to get back home as Shanae was due her feed. I drove home and when I arrived his mum and Pops were in the house. His mum had Shanae in her arms, and Jeevan was running around playing with his toys. I walked in and started yelling at Cassian. I was oblivious that his mum and Pops were also in the room watching at that moment.

"Have you contacted her?" I asked him.

"No, I told you I wouldn't," he replied. I then gave him another slap on his face as I knew he just told me another lie.

His mum then shouted at me, and I turned and stared at her. The expression on her face was full of anger. I stopped still and tried to take in my surroundings and realised where I was and who else was in the room with me. I looked down at Cassian's hand, which was now swollen. Cassian then left with his mum and Pops.

The next day he had come back home, and his hand was in a bandage. He had broken it and would need to have an operation which was booked for the following week. I felt so guilty and ashamed of myself for slapping him in front of his mum. By now, I felt like I had two people inside me. I had started to hear another voice in my head. The same voice that had told me to call her, the same voice that had told me to cut up his trousers, the same voice that had told me to physically and verbally abuse him. Then there was my own voice, the one I recognised. I told him I was sorry for what had happened and how I had behaved and promised I would never do that again and that he needed to go and stay at his mum's, at least until he had had his operation. I didn't feel like he felt safe around me anymore or what I was now capable of. He refused and said no, he would be ok and we will get past all of this. He didn't want to go anywhere. This was his home. He said he was sorry and that he would never do that again and that the call on his phone was from ages ago and not recent and that she had called him. I said to him,

197

how would you feel if I had done this to you with another man? And he admitted he wouldn't like it. *"Why did you spend twelve years with me and have children with me if this is what you were going to do to me?"* he looked confused and shook his head and said, *"I always wanted my children with you."*

I said to him, *"I am someone's daughter, someone's sister, and now someone's mother, and you have a daughter of your own now. Look what you have done to me."* He said he didn't know what he was doing, and he messed up. I asked him again if he had slept with her, and he still denied it. I looked into his eyes and could see he was still lying. Nothing he said made any sense to me at this point.

I then told him he had no choice but to go to his mum's, just for a week and that we both needed some space.

Eventually, he packed some things and hugged Jeevan and Shanae, telling them he would be home soon. As he walked out the front door, I stood there staring at him. He turned and said, *"I love you, you know."* My eyes filled up, and I replied, *"Cassian, you don't know what love is."* Then

I shut the door.

That week was peaceful somehow as I didn't have to cook for him or wash and iron his clothes. I had more time for myself and the children. Jeevan would ask where his daddy was, and I would say he is at Grandma's as his hand is poorly, and he will be back soon. My evenings were much more peaceful, and it gave me time to think. I knew I didn't want this life with Cassian anymore. I was trapped and felt like now I was in an arranged marriage and would be expected to stay with him forever now that we had children together. One evening, I was so upset as the time was nearing for him to come back that I decided I couldn't do this anymore that there was no way out for me, so I put the children to bed, walked down the stairs, and picked up a knife. I walked into the garden and sat down, and started to scrape it against my wrist.

I looked at my wrist and my veins. I was trying to build up the courage to cut my wrist. I would stop and start-stop and start over and over again. I felt I couldn't be the mother I wanted to be anymore and that my life was over now. I would just be his slave if I were to live another day.

The voice in my head would say, *"Do it, and then it will all be over."*

Another voice would say, *"What about the children? They need you."*

I was torn between the two voices. I had managed to graze my wrist at this point, and it was starting to bleed. I couldn't feel any pain. I was ready to go deeper when I heard the word *"Mummy."* I dropped the knife and ran into the house. Jeevan was at the top of the stairs, upset, saying he couldn't sleep without his daddy. I ran up unlocked the stair gate and scooped him up into my arms and said, *"That's because mummy is going to sleep with you tonight."* I fell asleep with Jeevan and felt ashamed of myself; I had never once thought if I had succeeded and if Jeevan had found me what effect it would have had on him.

The next day I decided to call Charlotte and tell her that if she loved Cassian, she could have him. I was a big believer in love, and after all, I had had my own love story. I was not going to get in the way of theirs, no matter how much it hurt. I also knew that when you try to stop two people from seeing each other, they would only want to see one another more. When she picked up the call, it was as if she knew I would be calling. She said that Cassian made a mistake and that it was only one kiss, nothing more and that it didn't mean anything. She said that it was a mistake and that she had left work so that she wouldn't be seeing him again.

Charlotte said he loved me, and it was me who he wanted to be with and that I needed to forgive him. I cried on that call. I told her about my ectopic pregnancy and how he had wanted to have children just as much as I did. I told her we had been together for twelve years now and what we had been through. After the call ended, I felt some relief knowing that it was over between them and that maybe he had made a mistake, and I needed to find it in me to forgive him. My parents left for Malaysia during this time, and Cassian and I had sat and discussed that we would tell everyone he had hurt his hand at work when they asked. We couldn't tell anyone the truth of what was really happening in our lives.

I started to go out clubbing with my friends now and carried on drinking and smoking whenever I was out. Cassian would wait up for me, and I would stroll in drunk and go straight to bed. I also stopped breastfeeding Shanae as I knew I wasn't taking care of myself anymore, and it would be unfair to keep feeding her my breast milk. I wasn't ready to give up alcohol. My weight had dropped dramatically in a matter of months. I never felt hungry anymore; food just didn't appeal to me. I could barely sleep at night unless I were drunk. Otherwise, I would spend my nights engrossed in my thoughts and think of ways I could escape. I seriously felt like I was in jail. We would put on an act for our family members whenever they came to visit and pretend that we were happy. That would consume a lot of my energy. Afterwards, I would go into the bathroom, sit on the floor and cry into my hands.

Our tenancy at the property was up for renewal. Initially, we had to take six months and now could renew for a year. Cassian asked me when we would be renewing it.

"We are not," I told him.

"Huh?"

"The children and I are moving out," I informed him. He was shocked.

"No, we would renew another year," he insisted.

"If I have to stay with you any longer than I have to, I will be dead."

I told him that the Cassian I once knew and loved was now dead, and I was mourning him. I told him that he was an imposter who had taken Cassian's place, and I could never be with him ever again. Dead people don't come back. We only have their memories. The following month I left with the children and moved into my parent's house with my brother.

Chapter 17

Betrayal

Shanae was eight months old when I left and moved into my parents' house. My brother didn't ask many questions. I just told him we would be staying for a while, and Cassian would be staying at his mum's. I called my parents and told them that we had moved into their house until we found another place. I lied to them and told them Cassian was living with us too. My parents would call regularly, and I would pretend he was out. By now, I had confided in my sister. I couldn't hide this from her. She was already suspicious, and she knew me too well. She was naturally angry and upset and wanted to confront Cassian, but I persuaded her not to say anything. During this time, she was now my rock. She watched me break down almost every day and try to take care of my children.

I would spend some of my days walking down to

Cassian's mum's house so he could see the children. His family chose to ignore what was happening and just acted normal around me, so I did the same. Pops did mention that we should sit down as two families and discuss what had been going on. He said that he knew that's how Indian families did things when there was a family problem, how they sat down and talked about it.

"I didn't have an arranged marriage. I made my own choice. No one is coming to sit down with me. I'm alone in this." I replied. But I could see that he was just trying to help. I also didn't want to hear any more lies from Cassian.

I did get support from Cassian's dad and his family during this time. He had come to see me one day and said he wanted to talk to me as he noticed on a few occasions that I was not myself, and I looked sad. I tried to reassure him that it was nothing, but he wouldn't stop asking me, and I broke down. I told him what had been happening and what his son had been up to. He was furious and tried to leave to find Cassian, but I tried to stop him.

"No, he's been through enough," I pleaded with him

and said that he needed to be there for his son and not against him and that his son needed him now more than he ever did. I told him how I had been hitting Cassian for months now. But his dad was not interested, and before he left, he hugged me and told me that everything would be okay and not to cry. If anything, I was now afraid that Cassian would be angry at me for telling his dad. He had a lot of respect for his dad.

His dad would come over frequently to check on the children and me. He adored them, Jeevan would go running over to him and jump into his arms, and Shanae would get excited too. He told me that I was his daughter, and he would step up if his son didn't and make sure that we would be taken care of. I could feel his pain, he had tried to talk to Cassian, but he had told him lies too. His dad would come and take his grandchildren to his house some days so I could have a break. I would open a bottle of wine and spend my day getting drunk and breaking down. My head would pound after, and I would feel even worse.

My friends started visiting me regularly now, and I

confided in them too about what was happening. I just couldn't keep lying anymore. They were upset that this was happening to me and disappointed in Cassian. They tried their best to support me.

It wasn't until three months later when Cassian asked me to bring his passport over to him. It was his birthday, and I had also gone over and took some gifts for him. He said, *"I didn't think I would get anything this year."* I thought about not getting him anything, but I didn't have it in me to be spiteful like that. I sat down at the dining table at his mum's house, and I remember feeling like I didn't belong there anymore and wondered if I ever truly had. By now, Cassian would just try and change the subject every time I tried to talk about our situation and how we would need to move forward.

The next day I had booked to have a tattoo done on my upper arm. I was feeling lost. I felt like I didn't know who I was anymore. I was questioning everything I had ever experienced in my life. Still, the one thing I had always known and felt was that we as people were all equal. But recently, I had started to look at people differently because of the colour of their skin, culture, or religion. My tattoo would be my first and only tattoo, I told myself. I was to have the Sikh symbol '*Ek Onkar,*' which signifies that *'God is one.'* This was to keep me grounded and remind me of who I was whenever I felt like this. A few hours before my appointment, a friend of mine came to see me and told me she needed to tell me something. I was standing at this point and started feeling anxious. She asked me if I knew a girl called Sharone.

"No," I said. She told me that this girl lived near Cassian's mum's place and he had been seen with her several times by people. At this point, I dropped to the ground, and it was as if my insides were ripping apart inside me. I had to hold my stomach. I burst into tears and could barely get my words out.

My friend tried to get me up, but I pushed her away and told her to leave me for a minute. Everything that had been happening flashed before my eyes. The text message, the name 'Sha.' It was her. He had been lying and cheating on me with a girl who lived right down the road from us. I felt humiliated and full of vengeance. I tried getting up but didn't have the energy at first. It wasn't until an image of my mum flashed before my eyes, and I recalled how she had fallen to the ground that day I had told her about me dating Cassian and how we hadn't helped her up, and she had got up by herself. This gave me the strength to get myself up off the floor, and I told my friend I would be back. She tried to stop me from leaving, but I told her I needed to go.

I drove down to Cassian's mum's house full of rage, and with all the evidence, I now needed to confront him. He could not lie to me any longer; I had suffered enough. I still had a house key and let myself in. Cassian was just walking up the stairs. He was home alone.

"Who is Sharone?" I demanded. He stopped halfway at the stairs.

"Oh, she's just a friend,"

"Another lie," I thought, and I charged at him. This time he said, *"No, I am not having this anymore. You can't keep putting your hands on me."* However, that did little to

dissuade me. We fought one another; I was screaming and shouting, and he was shouting back at me.

I managed to grab his phone and smashed it, throwing it under the cooker. I ran out of the house and jumped into my car, and drove off. I parked up where I thought he wouldn't find me. The adrenaline in my body was rising at speeds I had never experienced before, and I had to keep taking my inhaler. I made a call to a friend of mine. I asked him to tell me who Sharone was. I knew he would know.

My friend told me everything I needed to know. Sharone had two little boys with a lad that had also gone to school with us, but they were separated. She was almost ten years younger than Cassian, and now I knew where she lived and what car she drove. I drove to her house and parked across the road staring at her house. Her car wasn't there, so I decided to wait for her and beat the living daylights out of her. I sat in the car smoking a cigarette one after the other. The voices in my head were back. Thirty minutes later, I was still sitting there and then thought to myself, *"What are you doing? Look at you. You look like a crazy person. This isn't you."* I drove to Cassian's sister's house.

When I knocked on the door, his sister and her partner were shocked to see me in the state that I was in. I had marks on my body, and they questioned me about what had happened. I sat and cried and told them everything. His sister was speechless and hardly said a word. They said they didn't realise that things were this bad between us. Her partner talked to me and told me not to do anything to Sharone and how I would ruin my career if I did, how I was a good person and had two children to care for who needed me more now than ever. I calmed down a little, and I realised he was right. If I hadn't gone to his sister's house that day, I really don't know what I would have been capable of.

When I returned, I told my friend everything. She was in shock and upset that I hadn't told her what was going on. I told her I needed to go to my appointment now more than ever. I had my tattoo done and didn't feel any pain whatsoever. I had always thought the pain from my operations and giving birth or breastfeeding was the worst pain I had ever felt but compared to the pain I was feeling from being betrayed, they were minor. The next few days were a blur for me. I consumed a lot of alcohol and cried constantly.

Eventually, I had to tell my brother everything. I felt so ashamed when I told him how Cassian had betrayed me. He said he would go and speak to Cassian, and I told him there was no point.

"It's over now, and no one needed to say anything to him."

My brother told me that he would support me in any way he could and that he would help me with the children. He also said I could stay as long as I wanted and that this was my home. We also decided that we would not tell my parents yet as they didn't need to know. They were having a great time in Malaysia, and my sister had gone to visit them. I called her and told her that I now knew the truth. She was furious and said that she would be speaking to Cassian when she got back and that I couldn't stop her this time.

I felt as if I was the talk of the town every time I left

the house with the children. I would experience anxiety and look around at people and think they were staring at me or talking about me. My body would start shaking, and I would feel nauseous. Even though I felt like this, I promised myself I would get up and get dressed every day regardless of how I felt and take the children out and about. They didn't need to suffer. It was summer, and they both enjoyed visits to the park, and seeing them happy was all that mattered to me.

When my sister returned, she went to confront Cassian. He met her in a local pub, and she told me when she was talking to him about what was going on and how he could do this to his children and me, she noticed a group of girls sitting at a table. She got up and saw that it was Sharone with some friends. She rushed over to confront her, but Cassian grabbed her and escorted her out of the pub. She was furious and ready for a fight. He managed to drive away with her, and they had a conversation in the car where my sister told him some home truths about how his life would be now.

After this, I decided to meet Sharone and talk to her about what had happened. I wanted to see the woman who had ruined my home. I couldn't even look at Cassian now and had stopped walking the kids up to his mum's place. I couldn't walk past her house now that I knew she lived down the road. Instead, Cassian would come and collect the children for a few hours and drop them back. Communication had broken down completely between us now, and every time we looked at one another, it would be with hatred. I messaged her, and she agreed we should meet the next day.

I dropped the children at Cassian's mum's the next day. It was a beautiful sunny day, and he was putting the washing out. I told him I was going to meet Sharone and if he wanted to come with me.

"No, I will let you both fight it out between yourselves," he said. I laughed at him.

"There will be no fight. She can have you; I don't want you."

He replied, *"Do what you want. I don't care,"* and as I left, he cussed through his teeth at me and carried on putting the washing on the line. My friend dropped me at the pub that Sharone had picked to meet, and I told her I would call for a lift back when I was done. I was nervous and had told Cassian's dad about the meeting. I would always tell his dad what I was doing and where I was. I felt like I needed to let him know he had given the children and me so much support I owed it to him to know that he was a part of our lives and that would never change. He wanted to come with me, but I said no, I would do this alone.

When she arrived, I had already got myself a glass of wine. I could not believe that this was her. She was nothing compared to what I had imagined. At this point, my self-esteem was so low I had this image of a model or someone who looked like a celebrity in my mind, and she was just an ordinary girl. She suggested we sit outside in the beer garden and led the way. I followed her. We sat down, and I stared at her face, and she wouldn't have eye contact with me at first. She spent a lot of time looking down at the ground. She pulled out a packet of Embassy Number One cigarettes and offered me one, but I declined. I had my own packet.

At that moment, I knew that his jacket had smelt of

215

cigarettes that day I had found the message when he had walked out to go for his walk. He had obviously been to see her. She only lived down the road. As I was looking at her, she started talking, and while I was trying to listen, my mind kept running away. I thought of them in bed together, and I felt sick. She then had a call on her phone, and I heard her say, *"It's ok, I am fine. You guys can go now."*

As I looked behind her in the car park, I saw a car with some girls sitting in it and then driving off. She then told me that he loved her and had told her he didn't sleep in the same bed as me. He had even said that I would be leaving with the children to go and live in Malaysia soon, and they could then be together and have a proper relationship. I listened and felt rage growing within me. She then asked me if I had had an abortion.

"Yes, I did," I replied. It was the truth, but I was shocked at how he could tell her about my abortion.

How dare he?

Who was she to know about something so personal?

I realised that she was here for herself to confirm the things he had said to her.

"Have you slept with him?" I asked.

"Yes," she said meekly with her head down.

"I don't want him, so you don't need to worry about that. But why did you lie on the phone?"

Again she put her head down. She had no answer this time. I continued asking her how she felt, knowing she had broken up a home and ruined my children's lives. She was a single mum and knew how that felt, and now because of what she had done, I was now a single mum. How ironic.

She replied by telling me that her dad had cheated on her mum, but honestly, that was no excuse.

"Didn't you learn anything from that then?" I asked her. *"You will never be allowed near my babies. You can have him, but don't go anywhere near my children."*

She nodded and said, *"I respect that."* She then lifted up her hand and said, *"I can count on my one hand how many men I have slept with."*

"Really?" I lifted my right index finger, saying, *"Here's my number."*

Again, she looked down at the floor. She didn't reply. I had also been in the same class at school with her brother and told her this. I recall him being a nice friendly boy at school, and she looked very much like him too. I also knew her children's dad, as his brother was also in the same year as me in school. She told me that her children's dad didn't see her two young boys. I was in disbelief that I was sitting here at the age of thirty-one, even having a conversation with this girl.

I saw her as a vulnerable young mum, and I felt annoyed with Cassian and how he could have picked a girl like this to destroy our family over. I actually felt sorry for her. I could see how he would have felt sorry for her too. She then asked if I wanted another drink. I was done talking now. I knew there was no more conversation to have, and by now, I felt more relaxed with her.

"Yes, please," I said.

She returned with a glass of wine for us both. We

finished our drinks, and she offered to drop me home. I said yes. After all, we were both going to Cheylesmore. I hadn't even told her where I lived in Cheylesmore, and she drove me straight to my front door. She had obviously done her homework on me like I had done mine on her. When I got in, I took my clothes off and threw them in the bin. I never wanted to see anything that would remind me of my meeting with her again.

That night I dreamt that Cassian and I were standing on a mountain, and I was wrapped in his arms, and I felt happy and content like I used to. Then all of a sudden, the ground beneath us ripped apart, and we were separated. Cassian fell to the ground, and I grabbed his hand. Panic rushed through my whole body as I tried to hold onto him. I looked around for help and saw a person in a black robe walking around in circles. I called for help, but they carried on walking round and round. Cassian was screaming, *"Help me up."* I tried to pull him up, and then he fell. I screamed, *"Cassian! No!"* and tears fell down my eyes. I looked around, and no one was there. The figure in black had gone, and the ground had closed back up.

I woke up crying and punching my pillow. I was angry with myself. I was angry with God and the whole world. I was heartbroken God had given me what I had asked for and then taken it away from me, and that hurt. I couldn't save him; I had let him fall, and he was asking me for help. After a few moments, I calmed down and thought of that person in the black robe and who it could have been, and Sharone came straight to my mind. I knew it was her. She was waiting for him. I felt it. I knew from this point on he was gone now, and she had taken him.

A few nights later, I saw Cassian in my dream again, this time with a baby girl. It wasn't Shanae, as this baby was light-skinned and looked like Sharone. I woke up and realised that they would have a daughter.

Chapter 18

Retaliation

After the pieces of the puzzle had finally come together, I could now see clearly what had been unfolding before my eyes. Cassian didn't expect to get caught. He had not prepared for what the aftermath would be. I had no control over my feelings and emotions, and my reactions had been something even I had never dreamt of. I realised that all those months I had been pushing him away; there was a point where he had tried to make it better but realised that I would never be able to forgive him or go back to the way things were.

He knew if he spoke the words that he had slept with another woman, I would never return. I could see how his one lie had led to another and then another, and he had dug himself a hole that now he couldn't get out of. He had made the choice that he would rather go deeper into that hole than walk out, telling the truth and setting us all free. This would involve lying not just to me but to his own family too.

I could see clearly how Sharone now had the upper hand and become his source of comfort in this situation and why he was confiding in her. I was now the *other* person in this story and had been for a while. He was laying out his bed as he knew he couldn't be alone, and she was happily waiting for him without any care or consideration for me, my children, and our families. I called him and told him I needed to speak to him. He refused to come.

First, he said he didn't want another fight. By now, all the fight that was in me had diminished. I had no desire to lash out anymore. I now know the truth. I told him he could tie my hands to a chair and bring his brother or his brother-in-law with him so that he didn't feel threatened by me, but he needed to come and talk to me now.

I needed to hear it from his mouth, not hers. Eventually, he agreed and came straight over alone. We sat out in the garden as it was a beautiful sunny day; I had placed two chairs a few feet apart for us to sit on. He sat down, and

I told him about my conversation with Sharone. I knew that he already knew what she would have told him, but her narrative may differ from what we had actually said.

Yet, he knew me inside out just as I knew him, and I felt if I spoke to him face-to-face, he would know that I would never lie to him. I had always been truthful and honest with him, and he knew that. I told him I knew why he tried to hide her for so long from me now. I told him how disappointed I was with him. Why had he chosen a vulnerable single mum nearly ten years younger than him? The one question I had was *'why?'*

"Why?" I asked him

"I don't know," he replied.

"You must know because I have no idea," I insisted. *"I had been going crazy for months thinking about what I had done wrong, and I couldn't find anything."*

"You didn't do anything wrong. I just felt lonely," he admitted.

I couldn't believe what I was hearing. I was calm. I

didn't feel like hurting him; I felt I had done enough damage.

"If you had told me that, I would have put the babies down," I said to him, *"I would have asked my family to have them for a bit and would have given you all the attention you needed. But you chose to lie and cheat on me instead. That was just an excuse."*

We spent ten years together before Jeevan was born, and I thought now we will focus on raising our family, and when they are grown up, we'll then have that time to grow old together.

"Remember, how we used to say when we become old, we will sit on a bench, me wearing my salwar kameez and trainers and you wearing a suit with a hat and a walking stick looking at our grandchildren playing and saying to one another, 'we did it.'" I reminded him.

He put his head down like he had forgotten and was trying to remember.

"Have you slept with her?" I asked him. He kept his head down, took a few deep breaths, and said, *"Yes."*

224

"Is she the only one, or have you cheated before?

"Just her."

"Ok, thanks for being honest."

I felt deeply hurt, but I felt relief too. Ten months - it took me that long to hear the words from the day I begged him at his feet to tell me the truth. He had watched me suffer, and that hurt me more. He watched me fall apart day by day and, in all of that, doing my best to look after our babies and keep our family together. The words that followed next shocked me, but I felt I had to say them and that I owed it to us, our children, and our families.

I told him about my dreams. We both knew that my dreams were signs and signs I never ignored. I felt them as if they were real. They didn't feel like dreams.

"I saw you sinking into the ground, and you still have time to come back up, and this time, I will not let you fall; I will give you my hand and help you up," I told him.

I knew I would do my utmost to forgive him, but that would take me a very long time, and he would need to be patient with me as all the trust we had built up was now broken. He looked at me for a moment and got up out of the chair, and walked to the top of the garden. I waited for his answer.

"You can do better than me. I was never good enough for you," he said as tears rolled down my cheeks.

"I only ever wanted you, I never wanted anyone else, and you were perfect for me before all of this," I replied. But right now, he wasn't good enough for me.

"I should have let you go that day in the flat when you came to tell me it was over and we couldn't be together - the day I told you that I loved you," he said mournfully.

"Yes, you should have," I admitted. *"But you didn't, and now here we are. I will give you until tomorrow to decide, and I will meet you at your flat alone at 3 pm, and if you come, that was it."*

We were going to move forward together and get through this, and if he didn't, then I would know, and we would need to move forward regardless.

"If you decide not to come, you do have other options other than Sharone. You've spent a very long time with me, and being on your own may be what you need right now and to focus on the children, or you could meet someone else eventually," I said.

He shook his head and left. I spent the rest of the day telling myself that if he comes, I have to forgive him. I would have to make sure he didn't feel like I was going to hurt him. I could see from his face that he was afraid of me and would have to walk on eggshells around me. I would have to think of the children and our families who by now were also hurt and had no idea how to help us.

I thought of my parents and how they wouldn't ever have to know what I had been going through. Then I thought, *"No, he will do it again. He will think I got away with it, and that now he knew I wasn't going to go anywhere, he could do whatever he wanted."*

My mind kept going from one negative thought to another. I thought of Sharone telling everyone how she had slept with Cassian. I thought not once did either of them say they were sorry for what they had done to my children and me now that I knew the truth. They had shown no remorse; instead, it was clear that their ego and pride were hurt, and I was the one who had exposed their dirty secret.

The next day I dropped Jeevan and Shanae at nursery and decided that whatever the outcome, I would just have to accept it. If he came, I would learn how to forgive. I would do whatever it'll take, but somehow, I would do it.

I arrived at the flat at 2:30 pm, sat down on the sofa, and waited. I was so nervous I imagined him running into the flat and into my arms and telling me that he was sorry for everything, and then the pain would all go away, and we would be happy again. I looked around, and all the memories of the two of us came flooding back. I cried into my hands. Then the clock struck 3 pm, and I recall my heart beating fast. By now, I was staring out of the window. I saw cars passing by, but none were his. I waited for 15 minutes, and then I left. I took a sigh of relief and told myself, *"It's okay. Whatever was meant to be will be."*

I came to the conclusion that we cannot force people

to make decisions when they are not yet ready to receive the message. We can only see what we see when we are ready to see it. This reminded me of when I ignored my mum's advice of not seeing Cassian for a year when I had told her about my relationship with him. I myself was not ready to hear her message and made my own plans.

A week later, I heard a rumour that Sharone had taken him away on holiday. Now I knew why he had needed his passport. I visited my doctor and disclosed my situation to her, and she sent me to the sexual health clinic to get myself tested for any sexually transmitted diseases. At this point, I felt ashamed and humiliated, and I was now worried about my health. I had only ever had one sexual partner, and I started to feel bitter towards them both. My self-respect was stronger than my feelings and meant more to me, and I told myself that I would always be loyal to myself. I had put Cassian on a pedestal and literally worshipped him when in actual fact, I should have worshipped myself. My doctor arranged some counselling sessions for me. She could clearly see that I was depressed. She said the sessions would help me talk about my feelings. I only attended two sessions as my doctor's surgery was around a five-minute walk from Sharone's house, and I would have anxiety just walking there in case someone saw me. I already felt humiliated; I didn't need to bump into people at the doctor's surgery. So, I cancelled the rest of my appointments.

Shanae was going to be having her first birthday now, and I was organising a party at home for her. My family and friends were a great source of support for me as they did their best to ensure we would have a memorable day and that Shanae would have a special 1st birthday. One of my friends had made a special cake too.

Cassian turned up during the party with gifts and with his family. By now, I was praying for strength every night. *"Please, whatever happens to me, just please give me the strength to get through it."* I didn't need to pray for anything else. I spent the day suppressing any feelings that I had towards him.

My family and friends did the same. I had already told them that they were not to say or do anything to Cassian or Sharone. I did not want to cause any more pain. Fighting or arguing with them was not the way forward, and I certainly didn't want to give them any more reason to talk about me. Doing that would only make matters worse. He carried on as if nothing had happened. I could tell he had been away. He looked fresh and tanned.

On the other hand, I had bags under my eyes from crying and had lost even more weight. There were times when I would have to go into the bathroom and cry for a few moments, then return to the party as if nothing had happened. We even cut the cake together with Jeevan and Shanae in our arms, and everyone took pictures. I hated standing next to him. I felt humiliated, knowing that everyone was looking at us, and they all now knew the truth of what he had done. But I had no choice and managed to smile throughout these pictures.

Cassian had taken away any choices I should have had the day he decided to break the bond that we once had. But we all sang happy birthday and enjoyed seeing the children playing in the garden, which gave me some comfort. When he left, I broke down in front of my sister. She knew it was very hard for me, and she couldn't do anything to make it better. I could feel she was in pain, too, watching me like this. I carried on, letting him take the children to his mum's and spend time with them there.

One day, a friend told me that he had taken the children to Sharone's house as she had seen them at her children's birthday party. I was naturally upset, and my anger came back, and I remembered the words I had said to her when I told her not to go near my children. And as one woman to another woman, I was under the impression that women were meant to empower one another, but she was clearly showing me that she didn't care. I drove down to his mum's house. This time his mum was there with him too. Jeevan was playing, and Shanae was in Cassian's arms.

I walked in and asked if he had taken the children to Sharone's.

"Yes," he said.

"How dare you! Give me Shanae," I demanded as when she saw me, she started crying for me. He refused to

give her to me.

"Give me my babies. We are going."

He then gave Shanae to his mum, grabbed me, and tried to throw me out of the house. I tried hard to pull myself away from him. I was holding onto the banister and anything I could find and shouting to leave me alone and that I am not leaving without my babies. He said, *"They are staying with me. You are not having them."*

"Hey, what's going on?"

His brother came down the stairs and asked once he saw the commotion.

"I want to take Jeevan and Shanae and go," I told him bluntly. He walked over to his mum and took Shanae off her, and gave her to me. I was shaking and felt scared. His mum and I exchanged a few words.

"You should have forgiven him. It was one mistake. He waited ten years for you," she reproached me.

"How do you know it was one mistake? Yes, he chose to wait ten years for me, but he made that choice. He

didn't have to," I replied. I then walked out and put Shanae in her car seat. When I went back to get Jeevan, he wouldn't come with me. He was crying and grabbed hold of Cassian's leg.

"No, I want to stay with daddy!" he wailed. I tried to coax him and told him that he had to come with me, but he refused. Cassian was enjoying this spectacle and smirking at me. I left and sat in the car and waited. A few moments later, Cassian brought Jeevan to the car and tried to place him in his car seat. Jeevan was really upset by this and then grabbed me by my hair and pulled it, saying, *"No, mummy, don't take me away from daddy. I don't want to go with you."*

I managed to free my hair from Jeevan's hand and drove off. I was in a panic now. Jeevan was kicking my seat, shouting at me, and throwing his toys at my head, and Shanae had also started crying again. I drove home, grabbed some clothes and nappies for the children, and then drove straight to Cassian's dad's house. I told his dad what had happened and that I was going away for a few days to stay with my friend in London.

He was shocked and upset by this and invited me inside, but I refused as I felt I had to go right now. I left and drove away. The children fell asleep on the journey, and I arrived at my friend's house, where I stayed for a few days. She had a young son, so once Jeevan was in the house, he was fine and playing with toys, and it seemed he had forgotten about his daddy and what he had just witnessed.

I was now afraid and convinced that Cassian had other motives, especially that he would try and take my children away from me. I didn't know what to do and felt frightened and very protective of my children. I sat and thought about how he had watched me self-destruct. Knowing I had had to stop breastfeeding because I was drinking too much and had not cared to tell me the truth. How he had lied and lied and how he had now started putting his hands on me in front of his family. He had shown no remorse at all. I thought about my suicidal thoughts and attempts and how I wouldn't be here today, and what life my children would be living with him if I had succeeded. These thoughts were starting to consume me but not anymore. I realised that I had to be alive now more than ever and continue being true to myself.

I was a mother before anything else, and my motherly instincts kicked in the moment I knew he had taken them to another woman and not considered my feelings about it. I was their mother. I had carried them for nine months. I was not going to let anyone near them. I decided he would now have to take me to court if he wanted to see them.

In the weeks that followed, I managed to get myself back to work—working three days a week. I knew I needed some stability in my life, and working would take my mind off things. Seeing students in the classroom was difficult for me at first. I would wonder what these young children's lives would be like when they grew up. I found myself praying for each and every one of them.

I would recall my own school days and how I dreamt of a bright and happy future. I would wonder what their lives were like at home and pray that they lived in happy homes.

Sadly, that was not the case for some of these students. As a teacher, I became aware of some of their problems, which made me deeply sad. At weekends I continued to go clubbing and getting drunk.

I enjoyed dancing. It would remind me of my college and university days, and I loved music. I would just drift off from everything that I was feeling and instead let the powerful lyrics of the songs take my feelings away. For a short while, I would feel free. Often, I would drink too much and fall over. I would come home with cuts and bruises from these falls. But I didn't feel any pain; I just thought they looked worse than what they were. At least no one had done that to me; I had done it to myself. My friends tried their best to look out for me.

My college friend, Hakeem, would come over and teach me how to box. He was a boxing instructor for youngsters in Coventry and had reached out to me when he had heard about what had happened. I really enjoyed these sessions. He would tell me to punch harder, and I would.

I would imagine Cassian and Sharone's faces on the

punching bag and really go for it. I released a lot of my negative energy through this and felt like I needed to protect myself if anyone ever tried to hurt my children or me. Cassian would come and bang on my door to see the children, but I wouldn't let him in.

I would occupy them in other activities, Jeevan, in particular, so that he wouldn't notice that his daddy was hanging around the house. Shanae had now started walking and talking a little. I found things like that hard to deal with as normally Cassian would have shared these precious moments with us. I had told him over text message that he needed to make contact now through courts, and whatever they decided, I would go along with it.

We were too toxic with one another now, and I had recognised that day at his mum's house that our children were seeing and feeling all of this, and the impact was going to be devastating if it carried on. I realised that we, as parents, had been in an abusive relationship, and our children would suffer if it carried on. When Jeevan had grabbed hold of my hair, I had promised myself that I was going to raise him to be a good man in society.

One day I was walking with the children to town, and Cassian saw me and pulled over. He looked like a mess. He got out of his car, walked towards me, and tried to grab hold of my arm.

"I heard you have been going out to clubs with men," he stated. I started shaking, and Jeevan started calling for his dad. Shanae was settled in her pushchair.

"Let go of me," I told him. *"We can't do this on the street. I can meet you at my sister's later, and we can talk."*

I called my sister and told her what had happened she came and collected me from town. She took Jeevan and Shanae, gave me her house key, and said she wouldn't be far if I needed her. He came a short while later, and we sat down to talk.

"You can't be grabbing me on the street like that and in front of the children," I told him. *"You did it to me,"* he said, and he was right. During the six months I had spent lashing out at him in the house we rented, the children were

there on some occasions. I felt ashamed when he said this. He had reminded me of something I didn't even want to think of again.

"I have been hearing from people that you were out with different men and sleeping around," he said. I laughed at him.

"Cassian, how long did it take you to get me into bed? Just remember that. Yes, I was out, and yes, I had both male and female friends, and I can do what I want. It is none of your business."

The children were fine and taken care of. That's all he needed to be concerned about. After all, he hadn't cared about me in the past year. Why was he bothered now?

"Step up and focus on being a good dad. Take me to court and get access," I told him. By now, I just wanted him to fight for his babies but in the right way so that when they knew the truth, they would also know that their daddy wanted them and went through the right channels to have them.

"I will only respond to that," I told him, and then I got up and told him I needed to go now.

I waited for communication from him and carried on taking each day as it came. My thoughts were now consumed with how I was going to tell my parents. They must be getting suspicious now. It had been over a year since they had left, and I was still lying to them that Cassian lived with me. I would avoid their calls now and only respond to their letters. Instead, my brother and sister would talk to them over the phone. A few weeks later, I was leaving my house with a friend, and Cassian pulled up. *"Oh great,"* I thought. *"Here we go again."* I walked over to his car.

"I need to tell you that Sharone is pregnant," he said. He had just gone to tell his dad's family, who had told him to tell me before someone else did.

"Congratulations," I said. *"It will be a girl, and you better make it work this time."* Then I walked off and got into my car. If it weren't for the dream I had, I would have been in shock, but I already knew that this was going to happen. I was just waiting to know when. I had also already

told him about my dream a while back about him fathering another child, and it being a girl, and he had laughed at me.

After this, I booked tickets for myself and the children to travel to Malaysia and tell my parents that their daughter was now a single mother. I would be spending Christmas, New Year, and my 32nd birthday in Malaysia – all in all, a vacation for five weeks. I was a little fearful that they may disown me when I told them, but I knew I had to face them either way. I told myself if I am disowned, at least I have my flat, and I can take care of Jeevan and Shanae, and I will accept whatever happens. I will just focus on being a good mother to my children. I didn't tell Cassian at the time; I didn't feel like he needed to know. He had other commitments now. I told his dad and his family that I would regularly call and stay in touch over Skype.

Chapter 19

On My Own

Have you ever felt so ashamed you couldn't admit being a victim of a life you never asked for? Did you ever cry knowing that things won't ever be the same again, even if you try to hold back the tears sunken deep within your soul?

For my mental state, at this point, I wanted to focus on recovery. I didn't want the victim mentality anymore; I knew I wanted to survive. Being strong was the path I knew I needed to take. My options were slowly starting to fade, and my run for survival was within my reach. The more I ran, the closer I felt to becoming a freer soul. I knew I had to tell my parents the truth. I had a thousand thoughts running through my mind, and I knew I had to snap out of it. I needed to come back to planet earth and build up the courage to finally tell them everything.

I flew out to Malaysia on three different flights and a 20-hour journey with my one-year-old Shanae and three-year-old Jeevan. It was not an easy journey for me, but I did it. We arrived safely at Kuala Lumpur airport, and it was busy. My parents were waiting for us there. As soon as they saw my face, I walked over to them and smiled. We hugged for a few moments. I tried hard to hold in my tears, although I did feel a sense of relief being with my mum and dad. I had missed them so much. I had never been away from them this long before. Jeevan ran up to them at once and gave them a big hug. My parents were known as Baba Ji and Nanny Mum by all their grandchildren. Jeevan had been in regular contact over the phone with them and over Skype, too, so he recognised them immediately. Shanae was very attached to me, but it didn't take her long to adjust to my parents.

My parents were renting a beautiful three-bedroom apartment in Kuala Lumpur, and my dad had bought a new car that he was now driving. They had access to a swimming pool, gym, and park facilities for children. Both my parents seemed ten years younger and extremely happy. They told me all about what they had been up to; they had been driving and travelling all over Malaysia and had even picked up some of the language. They had also made friends, and my mum's family was in close contact with them. My dad's back had completely recovered. He said that this country's heat had helped him a lot. He was so active compared to when we were back in England. They said they had no regrets about moving away and would buy a house in Malaysia when they felt the time was right.

It was so warming to know that my parents had been having a wonderful time together and bonding so well. When I was young, my mum had always moaned about my dad watching football constantly. He'd have it on every week, season after season, year after year, and there was no way of avoiding it. Funnily though, during this time in Malaysia, my mum's attitude towards football changed for the better. Instead of complaining about it being on, she took the time to sit down and watch the games with my dad. She would take an interest in the teams and their players too. They had been cooking at home and eating *roti* and different curries on most days. My dad said that the vegetables in Malaysia were just so delicious and fresh and, therefore, a great addition to his curries. The weather was just beautiful too, and the sun would shine every day.

I felt somewhat happy again. My mum and dad loved having the children around, and we ate breakfast, lunch, and dinner together. I all of a sudden started to get my appetite back, and I started to feel good again. They would ask me every day what I wanted to eat and then cooked it fresh for me. I would visit the gym regularly and go for a swim to cool off after, and my body was getting the love that it deserved. My routine came back as it should. Thanks to my parents for looking after me, I felt like a child again. I started to sleep again too. Day was day, and the night was night again for me. They absolutely loved Jeevan and Shanae and would take care of them, as all of it came so naturally to them.

I was building up the courage in that first week to tell them that Cassian and I were no longer together and didn't know when the right time would be to disclose it to them. I was afraid of setting the truth free. We were all enjoying time together, and my mind told me not to ruin this moment, but something in my heart was aching to tell them. I always wanted to make my parents proud, and I was afraid they wouldn't understand, but a little part of me had faith that if they loved me, they would understand my pain. But I myself was finding it hard to grasp. Not only had Cassian and I separated, but on top of all of that, he was having a baby with another woman.

During the second week, my dad informed us that he had booked a resort in Kuantan for us to spend a week at the seafront. I was wowed and thought that it was lovely. I felt spoiled by my dad. We packed our bags, and dad drove for two hours to get us there. Kuantan is such a beautiful place. The resort was amazing, and we would spend our time eating out, sunbathing, and swimming. Shanae took her first steps on the beach and had a little splash in the ocean here. My mum took photos of Shanae with me on the beach, and I reminisced about the first time that Jeevan had experienced the ocean breeze in Jamaica with his dad. I often floated in and out of thoughts like this.

One day my mum said that my dad would relax in the hotel whilst the children had their nap, and we would go shopping, get a massage, and grab a drink after. I was happy with this and thought it would be nice to spend some alone time with my mum.

"Maybe I will tell her now," I thought. She felt more like a friend on this holiday, not just my mum. She was different, more relaxed, and content.

We sat down, and she asked, *"So how is everything Bubbly?"*

This was it, I thought to myself, it's now or never. I took a big deep breath and told her that Cassian had been seeing someone else when I was pregnant with Shanae and when I found out, I left him. I also told her about the other girl who was now having his baby. My mum's expression changed instantly. I could see she was in shock at what she was hearing. I didn't tell her anything else; I just didn't have it in me to tell mum what I had actually been through. I felt that she wouldn't be able to handle the whole story and that this was enough information for now. I had always painted such a wonderful picture of Cassian to them, and I felt this was all they needed to know. They had treated him like a son, and I knew they would be heartbroken too.

I didn't feel like crying when I told her; instead, I felt like I needed to sit up tall and show her that I was okay. She then said that they had sensed that something was wrong. The first night I arrived, my dad said to my mum, *"She has lost a lot of weight, and something is wrong."* My mum had agreed with that observation.

"But don't question her," my dad added. *"She will tell us when she will be ready to."*

My mum never brought forth the typical *"I told you so."* Instead, she said to me, *"Well, what can we do now? We have to raise the children and move forward."*

She further said, *"We can't go back, can we now? So let's move forward. I would have done the same if I was in your position."*

She gave me a hug and a kiss on my forehead. I felt like I had been craving for my mother's touch for a lifetime, and she made me feel safe and loved. The conversation ended with mum taking hold of my hand and saying, *"Come on, your children will be awake soon, and they will need their mummy."*

The next day she spoke to me and said she had told my dad, and he said, *"Tell her to tell me that if she needs anything, all she has to do is ask. She is not alone. We are right by her side."*

I never spoke to my dad about anything related to my separation on this trip, and he didn't treat me any differently. I had promised myself that I would never ask my parents for financial help. Although I knew they wouldn't hesitate to help me, it was enough that they accepted and loved us, and I felt that this was their time now to live the life they both worked so hard for. I felt some relief knowing that my parents supported me. My mind was beginning to clear a little. Now it was as if a dark cloud had disappeared. We did so much sightseeing and visited my mum's family. They showed so much love towards Jeevan and Shanae, and I felt at home there. I had not felt like I belonged anywhere for over a year now, and here I was, smiling and laughing with my family.

On Christmas day, my parents had gifts for the children, and we made it special for them. We spent New Year's Day at Batu Caves. The memories with my brother came back to me. How we had had a great trip together the first time we visited.

On my birthday, my dad took me to the jewellers and told me, *"Get whatever you wanted."*

I refused at first, but he said, *"No, you have to, it's your birthday."*

I had no desire for anything anymore; I didn't see the point in it. I then decided I would buy a ring for my wedding ring finger. I used to wear a ring Cassian bought me when we first met, and my hand felt bare now that I had taken it off.

When I was eighteen, and in the early days of dating, I had been to a jeweller's shop with Maa Ji and saw a beautiful gold ring. It had a black diamond in the middle, and around it, silver diamonds were placed, which made it look like a flower. When I saw that ring, I had already given it a meaning. The black diamond in the middle-signified Cassian, and the diamonds around him were me. I knew I wanted it, and I asked Cassian to buy it for me. He didn't hesitate and gave me the money for it, and the next time I visited Maa Ji, I asked her to take me to that jewellery shop as I had the money to buy the ring I wanted now. She took me with her and haggled a little discount for me too. I wore that ring on my ring finger for twelve years. I had taken it off when I left England and decided I would give it to Shanae when she was older.

I brought a lovely gold heart-shaped ring that day, put it straight on my finger, and hugged and thanked my dad.

I messaged Cassian's dad regularly, giving him updates on the children. I had told my mum that I was waiting for Cassian to make contact through the courts. I wouldn't let him see the children unless he had the court procedure started. She didn't question me further. I don't think my mum could really comprehend the situation I was in. It was foreign to her. The family dynamics that she and I had been raised in were simple. However, this was now something a bit complex that would take her some time to get her head around.

Cassian's sisters would Skype and speak to the children too. On one occasion, they told me that Cassian was there and asked if he could please speak to the children. I didn't agree, and straight-up said, *"No."*

Jeevan had not once asked for his dad, and I had not had to hear him crying for his daddy. I did not want to upset Jeevan and remind him of his dad or let my parents witness this. I knew it would break their hearts to see Jeevan cry like this. There was nothing I would be able to do afterwards if Jeevan had seen him, other than watch him cry and try to console him only to get upset myself.

I also felt that his sisters would think badly of me, but I had to put my family first now, and I could understand they were torn themselves. By now, I had realised how I always pleased everyone else. I invested so much time and energy in Cassian and his family over the years, and yet when I needed help and support, I felt as if I was ignored by some members of his family. I also recognised how difficult it was for his family members as they didn't want to pick sides. But, in my eyes at that time, standing by and watching me destroy myself and not saying or doing anything about it made them accountable too.

I would wonder if they had known all along; I just didn't trust anyone. Yes, some may say I should have dealt with it differently, but when you are in a situation you have no control over yourself, you lose your senses. Looking back, if I could have dealt with it differently, I would have, but I didn't have the tools or guidance to do so. The only person who made me feel safe and cared for was Cassian's dad, but I also knew that at some point, he would have to forgive his son and move on.

I knew by now that Sharone would be introduced to the family as she would be carrying his child. I knew his family would accept her regardless because I understood how much they loved Cassian. To comfort me, I would tell myself that regardless of everything that had happened, one thing I knew was that our children were conceived with love, and no one could ever take that away from them or me.

When I left Malaysia, I knew my path had changed directions now, and I was now planning my next steps. I would focus on completing my teacher training and start saving to buy a house and settle into my new life. A new world, a world I didn't really understand, but I promised myself I would learn and do everything I could to raise my son and daughter to be good people and treat others as they would want to be treated.

When I arrived in England, Cassian's dad was the first to visit us. He asked us to come over for dinner the next day, and when we visited, there were many presents for us all at his house. I had gone with the children. I took our photo albums from Malaysia too, so we could show everyone. As I was going through the photos, the doorbell rang, and I heard Cassian's voice. My heart started beating faster, and my body started shaking; I hadn't felt like this for a while. He had turned up with his brother, and as soon as Jeevan saw him, he shouted *"Daddy!"* and ran into his arms. Shanae just stared at him; he scooped her up into his arms and gave her a hug and a kiss. Jeevan ran over to me, took the photo album from me, and started to show the pictures to Cassian. He went through every picture full of excitement. I sat there and stayed quiet.

After a short while, they said that they were leaving. *"Oh good,"* I thought to myself. I felt like I couldn't breathe while they were there.

Jeevan then started crying and said, *"No, daddy, don't go. I want to go with you."*

Cassian hugged him back and started crying too, and said, *"I want you to come with me too, son, and I'm sorry, I'm sorry for everything."*

I watched as they both cried. My heart sank. I felt awful at what I was doing. Everyone was standing there watching this. None of us went over to tear them apart as we all knew Cassian had to leave and Jeevan would be staying here with us.

Moments passed by eventually, Cassian had to pull

him away from himself and left. Jeevan was inconsolable after that. He kept asking me, even begging me to take him to his daddy, and I told him that I couldn't.

"Why can't you?" he asked.

I could see his dad and his family were upset too, and nobody spoke, as their eyes were filling up with tears. I then grabbed Jeevan's hand and said, *"Come on, let's take you both to daddy."*

I told his dad I would be back. Jeevan instantly stopped crying and ran to the car full of excitement again.

I drove straight to Cassian's mum's house, took a deep breath, and knew I was doing the right thing. I walked in with both the children, and Cassian was sitting there with all his family. I smiled and greeted everyone. They all said hello back and seemed pleased to see us. Cassian's face lit up; he was surprised. Jeevan ran straight over to him and then turn by turn to everyone else hugging and kissing them. I looked at Jeevan and saw how happy he was. I gave Shanae to Cassian, and he said, *"Thank you."*

I replied, *"It's okay; I will come to get them later."* And I left.

When I arrived back at his dad's house, I walked into the house, sat on the stairs, and burst into tears. His dad's family put their arms around me and told me that I had done the right thing. I never realised doing the right thing would hurt so much.

During this time, Sharone's ex-partner had contacted me, and we had had a conversation. He said he had found out recently what had happened. He told me about the relationship he had with Sharone and how he and his family weren't allowed to see his two boys. They were twins and were four years old now, and the last time he had seen them, they were only months old. I felt sad for him and their two little boys not being able to see their father. We spoke for some time, and I told him everything that had happened. I told him the truth.

I had still not had any communication from Cassian regarding access arrangements, but I would often see him drive past my house. They had their baby daughter, and I felt a sigh of relief. When I was pregnant with my children, I used to wish the pregnancy would speed up. But now, I had a different perception of why a woman carries a child in her womb for nine months. It was so someone like me had time to process what would be coming next.

A few weeks later, my sister and I were sitting in the front room, and I looked out of the window, only to see Sharone walk past my house, pushing a pram. She was literally a few feet away from my front door. My sister got up and saw this too. I couldn't believe what I was seeing. How cold-hearted was that? My sister was furious about this. I decided then I would move out of Coventry and start a new life somewhere else. Cassian had not shown me that he was serious about fighting for the children, and I had waited long enough. He now had a new family, but I had to raise my own family all alone.

A few weeks later, I rented a two-bed house in Olton in Solihull and only disclosed the address of where I was living to his dad.

Chapter 20

Amends

The first night I spent in Solihull in our new home, I experienced sleep paralysis. I had settled Jeevan and Shanae into their room together, and now, for the first time, I would have my own room. I had never had a bedroom to myself. I had shared a room with my sister while growing up and then with Cassian as an adult. I hadn't even entered this earthly plane on my own; I had shared my mother's womb with my brother.

I fell asleep on my front and then woke up sometime during the night. I felt as if there was a heavyweight on me. I tried to move, but I couldn't, and it startled me. I felt hot and tried to lift my head and arms, but I was unable to. I then felt as if someone was lying directly on top of me. I was scared; I only had control of my eyes, and it was dark. My heart started to beat rapidly, and then I felt a face next to my face, and it felt like Cassian's.

I realised that this was Cassian on top of me as it felt just like him. His cheek was rubbing against mine, and I could hear and feel his breath against me. Then I started to realize that there was no way Cassian could be here. I took a deep breath and started to move my mouth to say the word *'Waheguru,'* which is the Punjabi word used to refer to God, the Creator of everything, and a word chanted as a mantra to take your mind away from the darkness to the lightness. Ever since I could remember, whenever I couldn't sleep, I would repeat *'Waheguru'* in my head until my eyes closed. From a very young age, I learnt to say the first verse known as the Mool Mantar from the *Japji Sahib Ji* prayer, the Sikh prayer that appears at the beginning of the Sikh Holy Scripture of the *Sri Guru Granth Sahib Ji.* I also taught Cassian this prayer, and he would remain silent while I said my prayers before we fell asleep.

Every time I put Jeevan and Shanae to bed, I would also say this prayer for them before they fell asleep. At that moment, my mouth wouldn't open, so I used the only part of me I had control of and closed my eyes; I started repeating it over and over again in my mind. Moments later, my heart started to relax, and I felt lighter. I was in control of my mouth now and shouted, *"Go away and leave me alone. I am not scared of you."* Then I lifted myself off the bed and rushed to turn the lights on. There was no one in my room, only me. I grabbed my pillow and walked into Jeevan and Shanae's room and knew that I was not ready to sleep alone just yet.

At this point, I was still waiting for Cassian to make contact through the courts and still had nothing. He didn't know where we had moved to either. I had cut off all ties I had with most of his family and friends now. I felt that walking away from everyone was the right thing to do; they wouldn't have to feel like they needed to choose between us, and I had lost my trust in every one of them, not knowing if they had been a part of his lies. At this point, none of them could help me with my recovery. And recently, I had started to notice from their expressions that they felt pity for me, but I didn't need anyone's pity.

That same week, my Massi Ji and her husband flew from Australia to Spain. They invited all my siblings and our children to come and stay for a week with them at a villa they were renting in Fuengirola. We were all excited and flew out together. I had told my Massi Ji what had been happening in my life over the phone, and she was very supportive. Being around her made me feel as if I was with my mum. My Massi Ji was a great role model, and I had always looked up to her.

I felt blessed that she loved me, always accepted me for who I was, and gave me the best advice. We had such a great holiday. My Massi Ji's husband's family had also flown out with their children too, and they were so loving and caring. One night, my sister and I decided we would go clubbing in Spain. My uncle's brother said he would take us and look after us. We danced the whole night, jumping from club to club, and he stood there like he was our own personal body guard, not letting anyone near us and just letting us dance as freely as we wanted. We rocked in at 6 am, and my Massi Ji wasn't too impressed, but she still spent the morning making breakfast and keeping an eye on the children while my sister and I nursed our hangovers.

It was heartwarming to see all the children happy and playing together. They were all talking and walking now and had started to have their own characteristics. They enjoyed being in the swimming pool the most, and at times it would be a battle to get them out of there.

When I returned, I received a letter from Cassian; he had delivered it to my parent's address. Finally, he had contacted a mediator and wanted to move forward and see his children. He said he wanted to do this amicably. I felt somewhat afraid of how this would happen. I replied, and contact was made for us to meet in Coventry, with a mediator present, and make access arrangements. Unfortunately, this didn't go as planned. We both still couldn't stand the sight of each other. This was obvious from our expressions. We often started arguing in front of the mediator, and in my opinion, the mediator wasn't really doing any mediating. We had three sessions, and on the third one, we both walked out. I was at this point still coming to terms with the fact that I had been having a relationship with a man I never really knew. I was upset with myself because I had never seen any of this coming.

It was my niece's birthday a few weeks later, and we all got together at my parents' house. My parents had just returned from Malaysia. They said they were needed here in England, and Malaysia wasn't going anywhere; they could go back anytime they wanted. Jeevan and Rijkaard were jumping off the bin and pretending they were power rangers. My sister and I weren't paying attention and doing other things. Jeevan came running up to me, crying, saying his arm was hurting. I looked at his arm, and his elbow was literally hanging off his arm. My parents were upset with my sister and me and told us we needed to keep an eye on the children all the time.

My cousin, Jindy, was visiting at the time and accompanied me to the hospital with Jeevan. Jindy did a great job at consoling him in the car, and he had stopped crying. When we arrived at the hospital, he was given a bed to rest on. The doctors knew it was broken and tried to give him morphine for the pain. Jeevan refused to take any

medication. He started crying and said, *"I want my daddy."*
The nurses turned to me and told me to call his daddy. I said,
"I can't. We are not talking right now."

We tried again to give Jeevan the medication, but he
was adamant he was not going to let anyone touch him until
he saw his dad. At this point, he was even pushing me away.
I was in tears. My heart was breaking watching my son cry
like this and push me away from him. Jindy was also in tears
now.

Her parents had split up when she was Jeevan's age,
and she had had to go back and forth between them as they
didn't get on. I felt I had no choice and so I grabbed my
phone and called Cassian. When I called him and told him
what had happened, I felt like an incapable mother. He came
straight over. Jeevan was ecstatic when he saw Cassian. His
eyes widened, and his face lit up. *"Daddy,"* he said, putting
out his broken arm to hug him. Cassian rushed over to him
and said, *"Son, I've missed you so much."* They hugged, and
both had tears of joy. I stood and watched, and all I could see
was the amazing bond they had as a father and son, even

though they hadn't seen one another for almost seven months now. Cassian then helped him take his medicine, and Jeevan never resisted. He stayed with us at the hospital and comforted Jeevan. He also attended every appointment Jeevan had after for his broken arm. Jeevan was only four years old at the time.

When I returned to Solihull, I spent the next few days thinking about how I could make things better for everyone. I just wanted a solution that would work for all of us and one that wouldn't make my heart ache any more than it had to. I knew that I would be hurting and healing at the same time. I was lost in my thoughts most days, and then this one day, I had a knock on the door, and I saw two elderly ladies standing outside. I could tell they were Jehovah's Witnesses. They had leaflets in their hands, and usually, I wouldn't open the door to people I didn't recognise and just wait for them to leave. Jeevan and Shanae were watching cartoons. I walked over to the door, opened it, and gave them a big smile, and said hello.

They introduced themselves and told me that they

were here to share a message with me. I invited them in. They came in and sat down. Pat was the lady who spoke to me. The other lady, whose name I can't remember, started to play with Jeevan and Shanae. Pat shared her message with me, and I listened attentively, taking in every word she was saying. When she finished talking, I mentioned the word 'Forgiveness.' Pat then put her hand on my shoulder and said, *"Do you need to forgive someone?"* My eyes filled up, and I nodded, saying, *"Yes."* She then said, *"First, you need to forgive yourself."* Those words were so powerful I felt a jolt through my body. When she left, she gave me the leaflet, wrote her number on it, and told me that I could meet her anytime for a cup of tea, and she would be there. I met Pat on two occasions for a cup of tea after this. She had the kindest face, and I felt safe with her. I didn't tell her my story, and she never asked; instead, I let her tell me her message and what she believed in.

After this, I contacted Cassian, and we arranged to meet up at McDonald's for a chat. This time we didn't look at one another with hatred. If anyone had seen us together, they would have witnessed two friends meeting up. He brought me a hot chocolate, and as I watched him at the counter, I noticed how tired and thin he looked. I felt sorry for him; he had now moved in with Sharone and had a little baby, and her two boys now called him dad. I gave him my address and told him he could have the children every two weeks from Friday to Sunday. He was grateful and thanked me.

I told him he could only take them to his mum's house or other family members. They would only be allowed to sleep at his mum's house with him there. He was not allowed to take them to Sharone. He agreed with this. I was not ready for Sharone to have any contact with Jeevan and Shanae yet. I had decided they needed to talk fluently and clean themselves before any woman would go near them. Shanae was still in nappies, and they both needed help in bathing by an adult. I had no problems with Cassian's family caring for them.

If anything, I knew they cared and loved the children deeply, and I trusted that with the bond I had with his family growing up, they would understand this request of mine. Jeevan and Shanae would also meet their baby sister for the first time.

I told him it wasn't about us adults anymore, and he and Sharone hadn't thought about the psychological impact this would have on all of the five innocent children. He looked at the ground. He knew I was right.

"One day, they will grow up and ask questions, and lies can only stay hidden for so long," I told him. I would tell our children the truth. I had no idea how it felt to grow up in a single-parent family, and only he could understand Jeevan and Shanae's feelings as they grew older. I would try my best to understand and not make them feel that they were any less than any other family, but ultimately, he had lived his life growing up like them and that he would need to support them with this.

I explained how he had unhealed wounds from his own childhood, and because of this, our children were suffering and how none of this was their fault. When I left, he stood by my car door and said, *"At least I got to see you today."* I said, *"Yes, you did."*

"Sometimes when I am driving, I see an Indian girl with curly hair, and I have to look twice as I think it's you," he said.

"Lots of Indian girls have curly hair these days," I replied.

He then told me that the family was asking when I would come and visit? I shook my head and shut the car door, and drove away.

I was now facing the fact that it didn't matter anymore whether Cassian was in a relationship with Sharone or someone else. He would always be their dad. Our journey had ended together as a couple, and a new relationship would need to be formed for the children's sake. I now looked at it as a business transaction between two people. I tried to put myself in his shoes and understand his situation, but I would always conclude that family was everything. Being raised by a good family was the best foundation for any child, and I needed to continue this for the sake of all the children involved, not just my own. Children sense rejection, and this

271

can have a devastating impact on their futures. I did not want to become a person who wallowed in her self-pity and, in the process, neglected the children. Although I had felt cheated out of my own future plans, there was no way I would get any satisfaction from hurting others.

At first, it was very difficult for me to say goodbye to them when Cassian came to collect them for the weekend. I would burst into tears after waving goodbye and pray that they would be safe and happy. I was experiencing a completely different pain in my heart that I could not explain. I never showed him this side of me. I would stand tall and smile when he would come to collect them. I didn't want to show him my weakness, and I never wanted the children to see me upset either. I would comfort myself by thinking that if I were happy while they were away, they would be too. I would then spend these weekends clubbing or staying over at my friends' houses. I couldn't bear to be alone; I had to keep myself busy, as that way, I didn't have to feel the pain.

I so badly wanted to forgive him and her; I just didn't

know how. All I knew was that forgiveness was going to be a long process for me. I started by reading all his letters and looking through old pictures. I spent one evening alone and cried, reading every word and looking at each picture. *"All those broken promises have gone just like that, and what a waste of ink,"* I told myself. When I was young, Papa Ji used to tell me off for wasting ink and scribbling. He would say that pens cost money and we shouldn't waste things if we could help it. I now felt as if I didn't have any value and that my relationship with Cassian was just a lie, and in my blindness, I had taken my family down with me too.

My family still had to live in Cheylesmore and had to go about their day-to-day lives, and it hurt me to know that people would be gossiping and judging them now and not just the Indian community but the black and white community too. I lit a fire and burnt some of his letters. I did keep some for the children to read when they were older.

Jeevan struggled to understand why his dad wasn't with us all the time. He would cry when Cassian dropped him home. After Cassian would leave, Jeevan would spend time crying and screaming and then lashing out at me. He would kick and punch me during his outbursts. I would restrain him at first, but it was harder for me to do this as he got older and bigger. He would say to me, *"Daddy said you kicked him out. That's why he is not here."*

"No, I never kicked daddy out," I would say. I decided I wasn't going to lie to my children. After all, it was the lies that had got me to this point in my life in the first place. I would tell him that daddy was with mummy and decided he would also get himself another girlfriend, and that's not very nice, so daddy decided to go to the other lady and have a baby. But daddy loves you and will see you again soon.

It would take a day or two for Jeevan to be back to his usual self, and then we would be going through the same process again for the next two weeks. This went on for a few years of his early life.

Shanae would cry for me and wouldn't want to go. This broke my heart, but she needed to have a bond with her dad too. Every child needs a mum and dad, I couldn't deny them that love, and I knew that Cassian loved his children regardless of everything that had happened. During this time, they also met their baby sister. Jeevan came home one day and said, *"I have another sister, mummy."*

I said, *"I know, how lucky are you? You have two little sisters to play with now."*

Every child is a blessing, and I couldn't have any animosity towards an innocent being. She belonged in this world just as much as any other child did and deserved to know her siblings too. I started to feel as if I was now doing the right thing. I realised that I was the key to unlocking this new world for all of us. I felt a little lighter knowing that the children were bonding. And I promised myself that I would move on and do what felt right for me, Jeevan and Shanae. I knew every day was going to be a challenge now, and only I could make my life better.

During this time, Cassian's dad passed away suddenly. I felt grateful to have seen him on New Year's Day when I had taken the children to spend the day with him. Through my journey during this time, he treated me as his daughter, and I felt blessed to have had this fatherly love, especially when my own parents were so far away. I promised I would do my best to raise his grandchildren and make him proud. I put his pictures up in Jeevan and Shanae's bedroom so that they would always remember him. I told them that their grandad would be with them in spirit and protect them. I would miss him dearly too.

My parents visited me when I told them Cassian's dad had passed away. They asked me why I had decided to move away and be alone when I had my family and friends beside me. I said I needed to get away so I could think and just be with my children. I had been going for daily walks with them and enjoying time in nature. Not having to worry about bumping into anyone or worrying that people were staring and talking about me was a relief.

I had been teaching Jeevan how to read and write and was fascinated by how fast he learnt. Shanae was becoming quite vocal now, and she would entertain me with her dancing and singing. They were both thriving, and I was more focused on their progress. My family asked me to consider moving back and get back to working full time. They said they would help me with the children.

My mum said working would take my mind off things. My dad had never taken us to school, and now he was retired he would do the school runs and help me. He said they are my grandchildren, and this is how it was meant to be. The children were meant to come to this world and into our families, and it was up to us all to raise them otherwise it will be the children who will suffer in the end. He said, *"We don't know what was going on in Cassian's mind at the time, but when someone is humiliated, and they know they have done wrong, we don't humiliate them anymore."*

A month later, I moved back into my flat with the children. I started working full-time as a supply teacher and started my journey to qualify as a maths teacher. I now needed to find and create myself. I would now spend my weekends and evenings studying.

Chapter 21

Moving On

I had been living off the savings that I had accumulated when I was with Cassian. I was saving for a deposit when we bought a house. Since that wasn't going to happen anymore, I was pleased that I had thought like this. If I hadn't, I would have also had financial problems on top of everything else. However, I was now down to my last few hundred pounds and felt extremely happy that I had a roof over my head and a job. I could continue my life, not needing or asking for any financial help from anyone.

I spent a lot of my spare time studying and working now and taking care of the children. I started by completing the Teaching English as a Foreign Language (TEFL) course. This meant I could move abroad if I had the opportunity.

I did get offered work by a supply agency to either

work in Spain or Dubai teaching English, and I could have taken the children with me too as there were schools for expats there so my children could continue with the British curriculum. I considered this and mentioned it to Jeevan and Shanae and asked if they would like to move to another country. Jeevan shouted, *"No, what about my daddy? I won't be able to see him!"*

I explained he would see him during the holidays, but he got upset. So, I said, *"It's okay, it was just a thought we won't go anywhere."* Shanae, on the other hand, said, *"I don't mind, mummy. I will go wherever you take me."*

Looking back, I can see that I was just trying to run away from my life here, in Coventry, but I needed to keep the children's needs at the top of my list. They needed their daddy either way. I knew that if I did take them away, they might hate me one day for doing this. They were enjoying visiting every two weeks and seeing him and his family. I started to feel happier, too, knowing they were happy.

During this time, my thoughts would be consumed with my identity. I knew who I was. I had always known who I was all along. Growing up, I was told stories of how the Sikhs were warriors and how we had battled for righteousness and equality. This was evident from the stories I read of the ten Sikh gurus. We had given Jeevan the name *'Singh,'* which means *'lion,'* and Shanae, the name *'Kaur,'* which means *'princess.'* I now knew where my inner strength came from. It was embedded in me from a young age, and I just didn't know it or know how to use it. I let go of what the community would say or think about my family or me. I realised my community had many flaws, too, and wasn't perfect. It had no reason to judge me. My family was solid, and that's all that mattered. I started a new journey at this point in my life, learning about black people.

My children were mixed race of dual heritage, and I needed to do whatever it took so they never felt like they didn't know who they were. I had realised that their identity and race mattered and was a part of what made them whole. They would be on their own journey. By sending them to their dad, I had given them that start. I sat down and thought hard about what I actually knew about black people while growing up.

At school, we were taught that they were slaves, and that was it. When I was young, I recall how I went to a Sikh wedding in Birmingham, and I visited the gurdwara on Soho Rd. Soho Rd is a very multi-cultural place and has many black people and Indians living in that area. I recall one of my aunties telling the other aunties to be careful in Punjabi because they were wearing their gold necklaces and bangles, and there were black people around. I remember feeling frightened and looking around. This was why I was a little afraid of black people while growing up. When I met Cassian and his family, all that fear had disappeared in an instant. I never had to think about that until now. I told myself my children would not identify as slaves, and I certainly never wanted anyone to be afraid of them when they were older.

It was at this point I met a man called Tobias. He was two years younger than me and lived in Birmingham. He was British Jamaican, and we met on Tinder. From our first meeting, we were both mesmerized by one another. He had these beautiful green eyes and was handsome. We spent the day talking and sharing our life stories.

I found his life fascinating and really enjoyed our conversations. It made me realize that people were living completely different lives to what I was used to seeing. He had many Muslim friends and had converted to Islam, and loved Indian and Jamaican food. His being a Muslim didn't bother me. I had a lot of Muslim friends and saw them as my brothers and sisters. Modern-day India and Pakistan were at a time one country. We all lived together until the British took over and divided us.

We discussed issues such as race, culture, identity, and relationships. I told him I hadn't eaten Jamaican food for two years now, and he asked me, *"Why not?"* I didn't really have an answer, and I just shrugged my shoulders. The next time we met, he took me to a Jamaican food shop, and he brought me jerk chicken rice and peas. We sat in the car and enjoyed our food together, it tasted so good, and I realised that I had been punishing myself. He seemed to know every Jamaican shop in Birmingham and would take me to get

Jamaican food whenever we met. My love for Jamaican food was back.

Tobias often spoke about his life and upbringing. He had had a tough start to his childhood, and because of this, he was open-minded and would question everything. He came from a single-parent home, and I asked him why he thought the stereotype of Caribbean men was often negative when in relationships and marriage. Tobias began to describe the environment slavery created for many Africans placed in the Americas and Caribbean. He passionately described how men were regarded as property and not given the natural rights of every human in being a husband and father. He described how slaves were often forbidden to marry, and hundreds of years of exposure to such practices would have a lasting impact on the generations who followed. Though free, Tobias felt that the residue left by centuries of slavery and its practices haunted many Caribbean males. After twelve years of being with a black Caribbean man, it made me realize I had never really acknowledged these issues before. I didn't understand everything Tobias spoke about at the time, but he planted enough seeds for me to research and question the world we currently lived in.

I started to see that we as people were all part of a system that benefitted some and not others. I saw the impact of a system designed to destroy family structure was actually affecting every racial group. As a teacher, I could also relate to some issues faced by parents in today's modern-day slavery, where society had shaped parents to expect teachers to do the job for them. Most of us were slaves to a system created to keep us enslaved. Divisions and labels had been created through war and race to keep people from becoming united.

We read Vybz Kartel's book, *'The Voice of the Jamaican Ghetto; Incarcerated But Not Silenced,'* together. Vybz Kartel's real name is Adidja Palmer, and he is a Jamaican dancehall artist. We both enjoyed listening to his music too. I found this book very educational at the time. It really opened my eyes to the Jamaican culture and not just what I had experienced when I visited Jamaica. This was when I learnt that my children's surname was a slave name. I realised just how little I knew about black people and their history, and I wanted to learn more. I recalled watching Roots, a series about the slave trade, many times with Cassian, and I would cry each time I watched it.

I had to cover a history lesson recently, and the lesson was to watch Roots, have a discussion with the students and then complete a worksheet. I found it quite upsetting at the time. I also recall how mature the class was about it and how the discussion had been conducted respectably by all the students.

I knew my surname and what it meant, and where it originated from. I had an original Punjabi name. The identity of a slave was taken away from them, and it all started with their names. The slave owners gave them names based on the jobs they were assigned. I then came across the William Lynch speech written by a British slave owner in the West Indies during the early 1800s. This speech's credibility is disputed, whether it was true or a hoax, but it is a speech given to slave owners to teach them how to control a slave by setting them against one another and, if done correctly, would be in effect for three hundred years.

The part that really stood out for me was how the key was to make the females think that the males were weak. They would do this by tying the male to two horses and letting them run and tear the male apart in front of the females. When the females would then have a male offspring, she would be afraid of the same thing happening and so would protect the offspring and train them to be a good slave, and in the speech, it states, *"Keep the body, take the mind."*

Whether this was true or not, I now had this image in my mind, and it appalled me, and I felt sad that any human being could do such a thing to another human being. This upset me deeply. I also read how the strongest males were made to impregnate the women and make more strong slaves.

I further learnt how black people were kings and queens and how they had lived in tribes and ruled kingdoms of their own before slavery. I could now tell my children a lot more than what I was taught to believe at school.

Tobias and I dated for almost a year. We realised that we were better as friends. I was thankful for this experience, but it was clear that we both had a lot of healing to do and needed to find our own paths.

Not long after, I managed to get myself a stalker. I had been out celebrating a friend's birthday and stupidly given out my number to a man. His name was Ranj. He was a Punjabi man originally from India. I said to him we could be friends as I wasn't looking to be in a relationship. He was ok with this at first, and we would just talk over the phone here and there. I met him for a coffee, and he seemed nice enough. He also took one of my salwar kameez to get made from a friend of his who stitched.

My friends had told me to be careful. They said men couldn't be friends with girls. But I shrugged it off and said, *"Yes, they can,"* as I had male friends. I invited him for dinner one evening, and he said he would make a nice vegetable curry for us. Jeevan and Shanae were with me too on this occasion, and he turned up with a bag full of sweets for them. They were so happy and grabbed the bag. I was not happy as I didn't give them sweets, and I told him this. They got plenty from their dad, so I felt that was enough for them. We had to pop out and get some coriander for the curry, and so we all got in my car, and I drove to the shop.

I left the children in the car with him and parked outside the shop, making sure I could see them. When I returned, the man, who owned the shop, was standing by my car with the door wide open. I ran over, and he told me the hand brake was off, and luckily, he saw the car roll back and opened the door and lifted it before it hit another car. I thanked him and got in my car, and I was angry.

Jeevan and Shanae were out of their car seats and messing around. I asked Ranj what happened as I know I had lifted the hand brake up. He said they were messing around and pulled it down. It wasn't his fault. I said, *"Why didn't you lift it back up?"* He claimed he didn't drive, so he didn't know. That was it from that moment I knew we would cook and eat our food and I wouldn't see him again. I strapped Jeevan and Shanae back into their seats and explained to them not to touch the handbrake again and that it was dangerous. When we got back, my mood was just off. I wanted the next two hours over and done with. We cooked the curry, and then we all ate. After eating and tidying up, Ranj said to me, *"Why don't you drop the children at your mum's so we can spend some time together?"*

You know that feeling you get when you just want to throw up? Well, that's how I was feeling. I was not attracted to him and didn't see him in any other way except as a friend. I grabbed my phone and sent my sister a text asking her to call me and just go along with what I said. She called me right away. I told Ranj that he had to leave as my sister needed a lift. He was ok with this and left. My sister wasn't happy when I told her what had happened, but she said I did the right thing and can take it as a lesson learnt. I felt upset with myself more than anything because if anything had happened to Jeevan and Shanae, I would never have been able to forgive myself.

Ranj didn't take it too well when I told him that I didn't want to see him again. He would call all hours of the day and night. He was leaving me drunken messages and sending me sad Indian love songs. He would call and tell me he loved me, and if I didn't answer his calls, he would kill himself outside my flat. I got sick of telling him to stop contacting me and so started ignoring his calls. One night he left a message saying he was outside my flat. I dared to look out of the window and just put the children to sleep and went to bed myself feeling worried. I couldn't understand why he was behaving like this. I had never given him the wrong impression and barely knew him.

My friends did the whole *"I told you so,"* and *"Why did you tell him where you lived?"* I felt like such an idiot. They were right, and I wished I had listened to them at the beginning. I carried on ignoring him for a few weeks. Then one day I took the children to visit my parents and while I was there, he left me a message saying he was outside my flat and had my salwar kameez for me. I was afraid to see him, and I didn't care about my salwar kameez. I wasn't that desperate to have it.

I couldn't go home now with the children. I told my

sister, and she was furious. She said, stay here; I'll be back. I just said, ok. Now I know my sister, and out of the both of us, she approaches things differently than me, so I knew if she finds him, he won't be back again. She returned half an hour later and had a bag in her hand. I asked her what happened. She said, *"He won't be troubling you again, put it that way."*

She gave me the bag, and it had my salwar kameez and some clothes for Jeevan and Shanae. Why was he buying clothes for my children, I thought, and the outfit he had brought Jeevan looked like something he would wear. My mum walked in on us and said, *"Something's going on, and I want to know what it is now."* I had to tell my mum everything, and she was mad at me.

"How could you give a stranger your number and tell him where you live?" I was upset I knew she was right. I tried defending myself, saying I was just being friendly, and he seemed nice enough. She mentioned the children and how irresponsible I was being. She looked in the bag, took the clothes out, and said she would be giving these to charity

as we didn't know him and we don't need these clothes. I kept my salwar kameez, though. Reflecting back at this now, I can see that I myself was quite vulnerable at the time. I was quite clueless about forming new friendships and didn't see the real intentions of the men I was meeting.

I saw him again a year later when I was out with friends, and I froze. I told my friends that he was in the same bar as us, so they looked out for me. As the night went on, he was hovering around me at one point, and then he came up to me and said he missed me. I showed him my ring finger and told him that I had got back with my children's dad, and we had got married and were happy now. He said, oh, ok, and never came near me again the rest of the night, and I never saw him again.

After this, my sister and I took our parents and children to Disney land Paris. We had a wonderful holiday, and the children enjoyed spending time together and seeing their favourite Disney characters. We spent a day in Paris and enjoyed a river cruise and visited the Eiffel Tower. I told Jeevan and Shanae how I had been here before with their dad and how happy I was to be here with them now. I had created a new memory of Paris.

I had managed to pass all my courses now and had secured a position as a maths teacher in a Catholic secondary school to complete my final teaching observations. I was so proud of myself, and by taking my life seriously, I promised I would remain committed to myself and keep moving forward.

The flat was feeling too small for us now, and I still couldn't afford to buy a property on the wages I received, so we moved out into my friend's house, which had just been put up for rent. Jeevan and Shanae had started attending a Sikh faith school now. I felt that this would be the right place for them to be educated and continue to learn about oneness through the Sikh teachings. Although I knew it didn't matter which school they attended, I knew they would do well because they had me, and I was their biggest supporter.

When I met the headteacher, I felt it was important to let him know about our situation. I told him that I was a single parent, but the children did see their dad, and he played a part in their lives. I felt I needed to make him aware of this as they would be unsettled at times, and their behaviour would change frequently. He thanked me for sharing this with him, he was a Punjabi man, and I could tell by his face that he was a kind and humble man. He didn't make me feel uncomfortable about my situation; I could see that he had compassion for us. I met some wonderful parents at this time and never felt judged by any of them. I enjoyed the school runs too.

I was quite military in the mornings with the children. I had stopped watching television and listening to the radio some time ago now and only watched certain films and programmes. I didn't want Jeevan and Shanae to be exposed to certain types of news at such a young age. They would wake up listening to Sikh hymns, and they were calm. I would get them dressed and give them their breakfast, and while I went to get ready, they would have some sort of activity or maths worksheet to complete. Once in the car, they would take turns to read out loud to me.

I would then write and sign in their reading logs

before letting them out of the car. They both got used to this and would follow the routine. I knew how important it was for children to have a routine. I enjoyed going to work and being in the classroom. It didn't feel like a job to me, teaching was my passion, and I loved being around youngsters, knowing that I was making a difference in their lives. I told myself that I was a happy slave.

At this point, Cassian and I would just still exchange hellos and goodbyes when he came to pick up and drop the children off.

Chapter 22

Experiences

I started to understand that life was full of experiences and how we had to go through them even if we didn't like them. I knew that I would have to take small steps. I had separated myself from Cassian and could see myself as an individual now. I would now spend more time with my parents and wanted them to be proud of me. I took my dad, Jeevan, and Shanae for a holiday to Portugal for the week, and we all had an awesome time. My dad enjoys going for walks, and there was plenty of open space for him to do this. I was bonding with my dad, and I knew that he just wanted me to be happy. He would come over often to see the children and check on us.

On one occasion, my dad was leaving, and Cassian pulled up outside. They had not seen one another since Cassian had dropped them at the airport when they first moved out to Malaysia. I looked out from the bedroom window and saw my dad walk over to Cassian, shake his hand, and say hello. I observed that Cassian felt uncomfortable when he saw my dad, but my dad walking up to him and reaching his hand out brought tears to my eyes. I felt so grateful and blessed that I was born into this family. Even though Cassian and I weren't together anymore, I would not allow others to talk bad about him. I just couldn't entertain such conversations and would shut them down quite quickly. After all, he was once my happiness.

I had loved him, and he was the father of my children, and no matter what, he still deserved to have that respect from me. I already had to live with the guilt of breaking down his spirit with some of the horrible things I said and did. I knew that he would be the same as me. I tried to put myself in his shoes many times. He went from raising two children to five children and with a woman he barely knew. I learnt that the world I was born into had now changed, and I didn't want anyone ever to feel the way I had, not even Sharone.

I cried most days, and not a day went by where I didn't think of him. I hated myself for remembering everything. Why did I love so deeply, I would ask myself? Every time I tried to forget about him, I would be reminded of him as both Jeevan and Shanae looked very much like him too. I absolutely love and adore Jeevan and Shanae, and I knew that they loved me too and were dependent on me, which comforted me. I knew I had to be strong for them as I was their safe place, and they brought me so much joy. I did, however, feel as if I had a wound that was never going to heal. You only have one heart, and I was very protective of mine. I would often tell the children stories about us, and they would be excited to hear them and ask me more questions.

I found it very therapeutic talking to them about the good times I had, and they would see how special their daddy was. I knew they would know the full truth one day, and I did not want them to have any hate or bitterness towards him or Sharone. I would want them to be forgiving too and know that either way, they were loved and cared for by both parents and that collectively we had done our best.

I would frequently visit the gurdwara with Jeevan and Shanae. Some of Jeevan's friends attended the Khalsa club at the local gurdwara, and Jeevan asked if he could attend too. I said, of course, and would take him every Friday evening. He only attended for a few months because he would get upset that he never got a prize. They only gave prizes to the children who wore 'Dastars' This is the name given to a Sikh turban. He would cry, saying, why can't he have a prize and then decided he wanted to wear a dastar. He was adamant that I should put one on him, so I did, and he was happy for a short while.

On some occasions, Jeevan would wear it along with his kurta pyjama, which is a type of long shirt worn with a loose salwar by South Indians when he visited Cassian and his family. Cassian never questioned me. He would just say to Jeevan, *"Is that how you are coming, son?"* and Jeevan would reply, *"Yes, daddy."* Then he would say, *"Come on, then let's go."*

I stopped taking him to Khalsa club because it was

unfair and discriminatory that any child who wasn't wearing a dastar would not be allowed a prize, and I didn't feel Jeevan was wearing the dastar for the right reasons. There were times Jeevan would want to go to school wearing a dastar, and the teachers would help him put it on. He grew out of this a short time after. As he became older, he started to feel that he was different from the rest of the children. I would try my hardest to explain to him that he was no different from anyone else, but it was a struggle at times, so I decided it was best to just let it play out and hope that he would see things differently as he grew older and wiser.

I then decided I would put him into the Punjabi classes instead at the gurdwara. I wanted them to be fluent in Punjabi and learn how to read and write it too. I felt it was better to teach them at a young age. They understood some Punjabi but were always a little reluctant to speak it. Jeevan was six years old and attended these classes at first, and he enjoyed them. Shanae was four at the time, and she said, *"Mummy can I go too?"* *"Of course,"* I said to her. So, I sent her with Jeevan and his friends. I would usually leave them there and pop out to teach some students for the hour and the teacher at the time was fine with this.

A new teacher had taken over the class now, and I wasn't aware of this until now. When I returned and collected the children, I sat them both in the car during the journey home. After the lesson, Shanae said the following in the car to me *"Mummy. I'm not allowed to learn Punjabi."* I asked her, *"Why can't you learn Punjabi?"* Her reply was, *"Because I'm black."*

I said, *"Don't be silly, Shanae."* Shanae then started saying that the lady said this to her. I asked her which lady, and she described her teacher to me. Shanae said again that the lady had said, *"You can't learn Punjabi because you're black."* She got a little upset because she said we didn't believe her.

I was in disbelief that anyone would say this to an innocent four-year-old child. A massive part of me knew that Shanae was not lying, but there was also a part of me that just couldn't believe this would be true. I asked Jeevan if he heard anything. He said, *"I was sitting on the other side of the room, so I didn't hear anything.* " I decided I would take them to the next class and stay in the room. So, the following week, I walked in with Jeevan and Shanae, and the Sikh teacher, who was middle-aged, noticed me and asked me to complete a form. The children both ran to the table and joined the class.

I filled in the form, and she was sitting next to me staring at me, and I felt uncomfortable. I gave her the form, and she read through it. She asked me to write down the children's full names, which I did, and she asked me to write down whether they were brother or sister. I was a little baffled because they both had the same surname, so why would I need to write if they are brother or sister?

She then told me to make sure Shanae was wearing a salwar kameez next time I bring her and to make sure it was simple and not like something you would wear to a wedding. She stated she would give me 3-6 months to correct the dress code and that she would be willing to be patient with this. I looked around the room, and most of the young girls had dresses and tights on. She praised me for combing Shanae's hair back in a plait and said that no makeup or loose hair is allowed. Now, at this point, I felt she was referring to me, as I don't think any four-year-old would be wearing makeup. She mentioned that this was not a babysitting service for me whilst I went shopping in town. I explained to her that I was a math tutor and the last teacher was fine with this.

She didn't respond, and then she said to me, pointing her finger up at the ceiling, *"This message has come from the top. Everyone here knows all about you and your children."* At this point, I felt deeply shocked and started to feel upset and was holding in my emotions. I felt angry and knew she was trying to humiliate me. She then said she would try her best to sort my children out and put them on the right path as our culture is Punjabi. She said, *"Hopefully, they won't take substances that are bad for them when they are older."* I asked her if there was anything else she wanted to say, and she said no. So, I walked over to Jeevan, and Shanae kissed them as they were happy learning with the other children, and I left.

I sat in the car park, and my whole body had started

to shake now. I felt so angry and had to take deeps breaths to stop myself from bursting into tears. This lady had clearly been racist to Shanae and discriminated against me because I had children out of my own culture and because of my appearance. My heart ached to know in her short little life, Shanae had experienced racism and didn't even know this. Now I knew I had other battles to fight. I collected them both and did not give the teacher any eye contact, but I heard her telling the children in the class. *"When you go to school do the white children wear Punjabi clothes?"* to which they all said *"No."* She then said, *"So why do you wear their English clothes."* She ended by saying parents should feel ashamed of themselves for not bringing up their children properly. This woman clearly had a problem with my children being in the gurdwara and questioning my parenting skills.

After leaving the gurdwara, I felt tearful, disheartened, and deeply distressed. I had to explain to Jeevan and Shanae that they would not be attending that particular class again. Jeevan started to cry hearing this, as he was very enthusiastic when it came to attending the gurdwara to learn Punjabi with his friends. I drove to my parents' house and couldn't hold my tears in any longer, and I burst into tears. When I told my parents, they were upset and angry and said that they would be going straight down there and speaking to the gurdwara committee. I said no, I am going to write an official complaint to them first. I felt strongly that my children and I had experienced racism and discrimination in a place of worship in today's diverse society. I spent a week looking at the professional teaching standards that teachers must abide by in this country. She had breached most of these. The underlying foundations of the Sikh faith teach us a great deal about equality, something which I am a firm believer of. I felt better writing my letter, and a meeting was arranged with the committee and my parents the following week.

During this week, Cassian came to see me, his mum had now moved back to Jamaica and was visiting England, and she had asked Shanae how her Punjabi classes were going. Shanae had told her she wasn't allowed to go because she was black. I felt so ashamed that someone in my own community had behaved like this. I apologized to Cassian and told him that the children do not go anymore and I am dealing with it. I told him that my parents supported me and that we would have a meeting to discuss this further.

He said to me, *"I have already told my mum that I know Nin, and she will not ignore something like this."* I replied, *"I am dealing with it."* I felt very strongly about this as I would never want another child or parent ever to feel the way I felt regardless of their cultural background. I already had a friend from college who had also had a relationship with a Jamaican man and had a son. Her whole family had chosen to disown her and her son and played no part in their lives. My friend would take her son to the gurdwara and taught him about his Sikh faith. I respected her for doing this and couldn't imagine the pain she felt from being unwanted by the very people who should have supported her. I felt blessed I had my family, and without them, I would not have had the courage to be where I am today. Having them beside me gave me strength, courage, and determination, and evidently, this would also be embedded in Jeevan and

Shanae.

It turned out the man we met in the meeting knew my dad. He apologized for what happened and had told me that the teacher denied saying those things. I was upset because now I would be seen as a liar. But I chose to let it be. What else could I have done? I didn't want to upset anyone, and she was from a different generation from me, so I decided to forgive her. I had made the gurdwara committee aware of what my children and I had experienced, and I felt that this was the right thing to do.

He told me that we needed more people like me in the gurdwara as the generations were changing now. I had told him that there are lots of women and men like me who have mixed-race children or are from broken marriages and other faiths and to make us feel like we don't belong in the gurdwara when it's already hard for us out there in the world is wrong and not what Sikhi teaches us. If we don't feel welcome, then we won't come. It's as simple as that.

He understood this and was very sympathetic. He was more upset that Shanae was targeted like that at such a young age. He asked me to return with the children to the class. I said I would think about it. But I never did. I just couldn't risk that happening again to either of my children. We continued going to the gurdwara though, no one was going to take that away from us. There were so many genuinely lovely people there who would greet us all with a smile. I recall one of the Giani's, which is the title given to a baptized Sikh who is honourable and leads the Sikh prayers. His face would light up when he'd see Jeevan and Shanae and make an effort to speak to them. He would ask them how school was, and they would call him Baba Ji. It was heartwarming to watch, and I wished that every person who walked into my children's lives would be nonjudgmental and honourable like this Baba Ji was to them.

My dad took us to a Punjabi shop in Birmingham after this and brought the children Punjabi books and reading materials. He even brought them fridge magnets in the Punjabi alphabet. I then started to teach them what I knew. Jeevan and Shanae were happy learning at home with me. I tried to make it fun for them. I also made sure I told Shanae how beautiful she was every day and promised to teach her to love herself unconditionally.

I saw Shanae as my little Earth angel. She gave me so much joy and love. She worked hard at school too. Between her and Jeevan, I learnt more about Sikhi than I ever had at their age. Shanae would teach me some more of the Japji Sahib Ji prayer and some Sikh hymns. Her voice was so soft and sweet to listen to. It would make my heart melt to watch her do this with such sweet innocence. Jeevan would tell me inspiring stories about the Sikh Gurus, and I would listen intensively. I was learning so much more through my children. We are all teachers in life, be it young or old.

Cassian and I started talking a lot more after this. When he would drop the children back, we were able to have conversations with them, and on some occasions, the children would invite him in for a cup of tea and have *roti* with them. I didn't mind; I was happy seeing them all happy. I was getting on with my life studying, working, and saving to buy a house for the three of us and spending time with my family. I no longer felt as if we were business partners passing the children back and forth.

A new friendship was growing between us, one I didn't quite have a name for yet, but our energies were the same when it came to taking care of Jeevan and Shanae. Cassian was getting on with his life, and the children had told me that when they stayed with him, he had known the first verse of the Mool Mantar from the Japji Sahib Ji prayer and said it along with them at bedtime. They had told me that they were also teaching the other siblings Punjabi words too and they were excited about this. The children never saw us argue or fall out again. We were creating a new memory for them.

Every Mother's Day or when it was my birthday Cassian would make sure the children had brought me a card, flowers, and chocolate. I would also take the children out to get him a Father's Day and birthday card along with gifts. When it was their sister's birthday, they would also decide whether to get her a gift or put some money in her birthday card. Whenever it was 'Raksha Bandhan,' which is a Hindu festival where the brother has a protective band tied around his wrist by his sisters, and he gives them a blessing in return, Jeevan would also buy his sister the same gift as he brought Shanae and would get excited about treating her.

This was always some Indian bangles and mehndi so the girls could spend some time putting mehndi on one another. I now started to feel as if I had done the right thing. Taking them out of the situation from a young age was better than being subjected to living in an unhappy home. This was the best outcome for all of us. Jeevan still struggled to separate the two families, though, and he did attend counselling for this. Cassian was very supportive of this and would attend any meetings he needed to help Jeevan understand.

The incident with the teacher made me think of Cassian's mum and how she must have felt hearing from Shanae that she wasn't allowed to attend Punjabi classes. I know she would have felt deeply hurt hearing her granddaughter say such a thing to her at such a very young age. As mothers, we do our best to protect our children, and

311

looking back to when the affair was unfolding, I could understand that his mum was just doing what she thought was best in the circumstances. At the time, we were all dealing with half-truths, so it was inevitable that decisions and choices would be made without full details. I loved his mum dearly. I treated her as my own mother when I was growing up around her. I knew that Cassian was the apple of her eye. I felt I could forgive her and hoped that she would forgive me for slapping her son in front of her one day.

Chapter 23

Milestones

Life was beginning to feel purposeful for me again. Jeevan and Shanae kept me busy, and I spent a lot of time taking them away on holidays during the school break. We spent a week in Malta, a canary island, and they both loved swimming in the resort pool. They were also great at making friends and would be playing with other children in no time. We visited Fuerteventura, also another canary island, for a week, and they enjoyed time in the ocean and the lovely weather. We almost certainly would have to find a water park to spend the day in and find a local zoo. Jeevan and Shanae would already have the agenda ready for our trip and everything they wanted to do and see.

I was thoroughly enjoying my teaching role in the Catholic school. My day would start by sitting in the staff room with all my colleagues, and we would say the Lord's

Prayer together 'Our Father, who art in heaven, hallowed be Thy name, Thy kingdom come, Thy will be done on earth as it is in heaven. Give us this day our daily bread and forgive us our trespasses as we forgive those who trespass against us and lead us not into temptation but deliver us from evil. Amen.' After this prayer, my school day would begin. I would attend Mass weekly and listen intensively when the priest would do his speeches and tell stories from the bible. By doing this daily prayer, I found my day would feel less stressful, and I would have faith that everything would be ok that day. I worked with some amazing colleagues and students too. I was inspired by the dedication of the staff and students and felt blessed to work in a school like this.

The guidance and training I received from my mentors was phenomenal. They saw the potential in me and guided me, and I felt so humbled by their dedication to seeing me succeed. I also made many friends during this point who I looked up to and admired. I knew that I could be a great teacher who would correct pupils' behaviour too because I myself was living a life where I was treating people with respect and not making judgements. I would never feel any satisfaction from humiliating someone, and if I had to correct people by humiliating them, what would I be teaching the future generations?

I started to look at my life and realised just how blessed I was. I had two beautiful children; my family loved and supported me; my passion was to teach and help students, and I was doing this. I had saved enough now to buy a house for us and had started the process of house hunting. Cassian was having a relationship with the children, and they were settled. He never turned up late or let them down. If anything, he would now see them during some weekdays too and help with school pickups. At times he would come over and support me when Jeevan and Shanae weren't doing as they were told. So, when he asked if they could meet Sharone, I said, *"Yes, why not."* They would initially go for dinner and then back to his mum's.

This went on for a short while until Jeevan and Shanae started asking me why they couldn't stay over at Sharone's. I said I wasn't ready for that just yet. A few months later, I gave in. They stayed over at Sharone's and told me how much fun they had. I was pleased that's how it should be, I told myself. By now, I had met many families that were similar to my own and heard from people about their own experiences in life. I didn't feel so alone in the world now. I had managed to turn everything negative that had happened into something positive.

I thought about Sharone. She was a hairdresser, and from my experience, hairdressers are like your friends. They talk and listen to you while they cut your hair. At my hairdresser's, as soon as you walk in, there is a sign that says, *"Hairstylists bring out the beauty in you."* I would think that just because she had made certain choices didn't mean she was a bad person. We are all faced with decisions and choices throughout our lives, and we are all on our own journeys. At this point, mentally, I was in a better place, and I recognised that my life wasn't as bad as it had seemed. I was becoming stronger in mind, body, and spirit, and my tears were fading away.

I felt that I could forgive her, and if anything, I just

wanted to have a peaceful life and for everyone else to have a happy life too. Sharone would also do Shanae's hair for her, and I can admit that she did a much better job than me. Styling hair just wasn't my thing, and I would often struggle to do styles on Shanae's hair. I realised that growing up, I was trying to bring two communities together, and now, with Sharone's part in my story, I could bring all communities together.

I felt happy and content. I was meditating at home daily now and found deep breathing exercises to be very useful. In fact, my anxiety levels went down significantly. I would attend yoga sessions and then started doing them daily at home. I was learning to love myself and keeping myself out of situations that drained my energy. By now, I had recognised that my gut instinct was my source of power and that the universe was giving me signs each and every moment. I just needed to pay attention. Cassian had asked if he could take the children away for a week to the seaside, and I agreed. This would be the first time I would be away from them for more than a day or two. I then decided I wasn't ready to spend a week home alone, so I booked myself a holiday to Spain in Lloret De Mar Costa Brava for five days.

As soon as I reached my hotel, I had made friends. I was looking for my apartment and walked past the swimming pool, and there were four girls around the same age as me. I was thirty-five at the time they were sunbathing and listening to reggae and dancehall music. One of them asked me if I was ok and I told them I was looking for my apartment. It turned out my apartment was right next door to theirs. They asked me who I was here with and I told them that I was alone.

One of them said, *"Well, get your bikini on and come and join us."* I said I would think about it, and thanks for the offer. I walked into my apartment, which was nice and spacious. I sat down on the balcony, and the sun was shining on my face. I closed my eyes and took this warm feeling in for a few moments before deciding to get dressed into my bikini and join the girls. They seemed pleased to see me and introduced themselves to me; their names were Siobhan, Stacey, Janine, and Lee-Ann.

I spent three days hanging out with them and getting to know them. They were from Liverpool and celebrating a birthday together. They were single mums like me, so we shared our life stories with one another. Lee-Ann had asked me if I was black. *"No, I am Indian,"* I told her, *"but my children are mixed-race Jamaican."*

"Ah," said Siobhan. *"I knew there was something black about you."* That made me giggle. Stacey asked me why I was single. I told her my story, and by now, I had got used to explaining why I was single. I would say that I was with my ex-partner for twelve years, and we had two children, and then he decided to cheat on me, so I left him. It would usually be something along those lines. I also didn't feel as ashamed about it like I used to. I was at a point where I had no choice but to accept my past. There was no way I was going to let my past ruin my future. The girls also shared some of their own experiences with me, which I could understand. Janine took out her phone and started showing me pictures of her children, and the other girls did the same. I felt comfortable enough to share pictures of Jeevan and

Shanae with them too. I felt blessed to be sitting with mothers who had the same love for their children like I did.

I could see it in their pictures and from the happy expressions on their children's faces that they were great mums like me who put their children's needs first. There were five of us now, and we would get together in one room and get dressed up and dance whilst listening to music. I felt they had so much in common with me, especially our taste in music. We would go clubbing and just dance the night away. They looked out for me, and if someone were observing us, you wouldn't have thought I had only met them hours ago.

Our night would end up at a shisha bar, and we would enjoy sitting out on a warm night out on the balcony, just living in the present moment. Some men would try to get our attention and hover around us, but these girls were so strong-minded they made sure the men knew to keep away from us. I felt empowered being with them. They were like-minded and just wanted to dance and enjoy the evening like me, and no male attention was going to ruin that for us.

During the day, we would be sunbathing, sipping on cocktails, and listening to music. Later, we'd be enjoying dinner together. On their final day with me, the girls offered to take me to the shops on the seafront to get some souvenirs and gifts for my children. Siobhan had mentioned to me that they had been before and we could all go together. So we walked into the souvenir shop, and as soon as the shopkeeper saw us walk in, he shouted in Punjabi to another member of staff, *"Don't forget to charge these black girls double at the till."*

I was startled by this as none of the girls would understand that he had said this. Two of the girls were mixed race, and the other two were black. I think the shopkeeper thought that I might be black too. Well, I mentioned to the girls what he had said, none of them were impressed. We carried on shopping, and when he calculated up our shopping, I spoke to him in Punjabi and told him I had understood what he had said. He was gob smacked. He said he didn't realize I was Punjabi, and he was very apologetic.

He let us have most of the items for free. The girls

made sure they gave him a piece of their mind too before we left. I never expected to make friends on holiday, and they made my trip so much more worthwhile. I was in need of good company, and I felt empowered by their positive outlook on life. I was grateful for this experience, and even though it was short, the impact it had on me would last a lifetime.

My parents would call and make sure I was ok and my dad had dropped me to the airport. When I had told them, I would be going away alone, they were unsure about it at first. I explained how it was something that I had always wanted to do but was afraid of doing. However now, I felt I could do this. My parents understood this and said that it was okay but that I would frequently need to skype and message. I explained how I had made friends and was out and about with them, my mum said, *"Bubbly, only you could make friends with strangers."* She told me to have fun and be careful.

When the girls left, we promised to keep in touch. We exchanged numbers, and connected on social media platforms. I spent the last two days sightseeing and shopping alone. I felt like such a free spirit, and I enjoyed being alone in my own company now. I found myself smiling for no reason when I was lost in my thoughts. I was happy, and anyone who could see me would have seen nothing but happiness from me this time.

When I got back to England, I was ready for my next big and final move. I sold my flat and bought us a house closer to my work and to the children's school. I also decided to make a trip to India with the children, show them where my dad was brought up, and introduce them to other family members. So I started saving up for this trip. I also wanted to take them to Sri Harminder Sahib Ji, The Golden Temple in Amritsar. Travelling was something that I enjoyed doing and would look forward to throughout my life, and I wanted to show both my children as much of the world as I possibly could whilst I was alive and make as many memories with them.

I wanted them to have as many experiences as possible in the world as it is such a beautiful place. They deserved to see as much of it in their lifetime.

Our new house was just beautiful. When I first saw the garden, I knew Jeevan and Shanae would love it just as much as I did. They ran to the garden and said, *"Mummy, please can we have this house?"* They reminded me of my siblings and me when we were their age and had said the same thing to our parents when they had brought our new house at the time. They both rummaged through their money boxes and gave me their pennies, saying, *"Here this is towards paying for the house, mum."*

I smiled and took the money off them and said, *"Oh great, we have enough now."* I had the house, and my family blessed with a Sukhmani Sahib Ji prayer. This involves bringing the Sri Guru Granth Sahib Ji, the holy Sikh scripture, to the house. I felt so proud of myself. Through hard work and dedication, I had been able to create the best version of myself and be a good role model for my children.

To begin with, we would spend a lot of time outside in the garden and would do the gardening and plant plants together. We were also blessed with lovely neighbours. We lived next door to a couple in their eighties called Alan and June.

Alan was Scottish but raised in Ireland, and June was English. They quickly made us feel welcome and would often come over and see Jeevan and Shanae. They would praise me almost every time I saw them. Telling me how well I was raising my children and to keep working hard. I would thank them, and we created a bond with them. June would come over and help me with the gardening and teach me about plants and flowers. Alan would be my first point of contact if something broke in the house. He would come straight over with his toolbox and help me. Alan would also spend time telling me funny stories about his upbringing in Ireland. He would almost certainly have me giggling with his stories.

Jeevan and Shanae respected them like they were their grandparents, and June and Alan would often tell me that Jeevan and Shanae were no different from their own grandchildren. June would often come over and spoil them both with sweets and money. I admired both of them and would envision myself happy and settled in my own life like they were with someone one day.

I was now able to sleep alone and spent weekends by myself. Sometimes I would do absolutely nothing or just listen to music. I was embracing every moment I had now and making the most of it. I had grown so much as a person now, and life seemed blissful again. When we were enjoying time at home together, Jeevan and Shanae would watch Bollywood films with me too. They would sit still throughout the whole film. I would also have a specific time during the evening, which I called 'Bhangra Time.' This was where the three of us would just get up and let ourselves dance as freely as we wanted in the living room.

It was so much fun that we would copy the videos from the Indian films, copy the dancers, and sing out loud. By the end of Bhangra time, we were no longer making Bhangra moves. We would be dancing to either English, Reggae, hip hop, and Dancehall music. The three of us were happy and living in the present moment, and seeing Jeevan and Shanae smile made me the happiest mum in the world.

There were occasions Rijkaard and Khula would come over to stay, and they would enjoy Bhangra time with us too. Khula, Shanae, and I would practice and perform dance routines, record them and send them to my mum. As a family, we were very close, and my parents would often tell us to keep our bond strong and the children happy.

I liked the fact that my children were embracing both cultures. They would go over to their dad's, who would take them to family gatherings and functions. They would come back happy and tell me about all the tasty Jamaican food they ate and the family members they had met. I had more time on my hands now, so I decided to make them Jamaican food at home. One of my closest friends had brought me the Levi Roots Jamaican cookbook, so I got that out and started with ackee and saltfish. When the children were ready for their dinner, I served the ackee and saltfish. They were surprised. When they started to eat it, Jeevan said, *"Mummy, you sure this is ackee and saltfish?"* I said yes, then Shanae said, *"How come it tastes like a curry then?"* I started to laugh and told them that I had gotten carried away and thought I would spice it up with some Indian spices.

They both told me not to do that again and refused to eat it. The second time I made ackee and saltfish, I followed the recipe and dished out their food. They both spat it straight out. I had forgotten to take the salt out of the fish. I was not going to give up, I told them, and the third time I made ackee and saltfish, they both said it was lovely, and although it wasn't as good as their grandma's, it had at least tasted like ackee and saltfish. After this, I made them rice and peas, curry chicken, dumplings, jerk chicken, soup and oxtail.

Cassian also made them curries and *roti* too, they would tell me when they got back and say, *"Daddy made roti, but it wasn't as good as yours, mummy."* I replied by saying, *"Look, at least we both try."*

There were times that Sharone had come to collect the children. Cassian would always message me beforehand and let me know this. I was fine with it, and I felt respected enough to know he had let me know. The first time this happened, Jeevan said to me, *"Mum, you don't need to wave at us today."* I said, *"Why not? I always wave, and I will continue to do so."* I could see from their expressions that they both felt awkward that Sharone and I would see each other. I actually didn't mind at all. When she pulled up outside in her car, I waved and smiled at her, and she waved and smiled back. When they came home the next day, they both told me that it was nice seeing us waving to one another. Wonderful, I thought now they didn't have to feel awkward anymore.

I had now come to the end of my teaching observations, and after working as a part-qualified maths teacher for a number of years now, I had finished my teaching qualification and was now a fully qualified maths teacher. I was very proud of myself, so was my family. They knew how hard I had worked to achieve this goal of mine. It had taken me longer than anticipated, but I had done it. I celebrated with my family by going out for dinner one evening. Jeevan and Shanae told me how proud they were of me, too, and hearing that come from their mouths made every second of it worthwhile.

Before we left for India, I attended a reiki session. I

had never had this experience before and was now following a more spiritual path in life. I was finally in tune with myself and needed to stay grounded at all times. I was now living my life in the present moment, not worrying about the past or the future. I knew, either way, I would always be taken care of. During reiki, I experienced a vision that helped me go back and comfort my inner child throughout every significant moment in my life and forgive myself for my choices and decisions growing up. I envisioned that I was in a beautiful green field in India, and I saw Cassian sitting on a cart. It was the Cassian I had once known I could tell from his eyes.

He had a peaceful smile on his face. The cart was moving away in the opposite direction of me, and I smiled back at him, and we both waved goodbye to one another; I was ready to let him go now and felt happy inside while I was waving. When he had disappeared into the fields, I saw a figure running towards me from afar with their arms out. I waited for them to come closer as I couldn't quite make out who it was, when they came closer I realised that it was me.

I was standing watching myself, and I pulled out my arms and ran towards me. I hugged myself tightly. I felt immense relief and happiness that it made me cry. I now knew that it was me all along.

I had to love myself. The lady who was with me in the room carrying out the reiki told me that she could see I had a lot of pain in my heart and that I needed to put myself first. She didn't know anything about me but told me that I was on a journey of self-love. She told me that I was a free spirit, and it saddened her to see me trapped but that I didn't need to be anymore. I was able to forgive myself for making choices from a place of not knowing my own worth and take responsibility for my own actions now. I would travel back during my meditation and comfort myself now that I knew how and at each stage in my life where I felt there was pain. I would tell my inner child that I had forgiven myself that I didn't know any better then, but I do now, and everything would be ok now.

This process helped me to release any negativity I had around me too. I now knew that the road ahead was going to be a good one. I had no regrets when it came to having my children, they were gifted to me, and I was meant to be their mother, and I, therefore, could not go back to the time I had met Cassian. I did not see this as a negative it was a blessing with him. I would never have become the person I was becoming.

The relationship we had taught me what love was, and I still felt fortunate that I had been blessed with such love at one time in my life. I wanted nothing more for him except to be happy and content and at peace with himself, too. I truly hoped that he could also forgive himself for what he had done to his family. We were Jeevan and Shanae's parents, and this was a bond that had proved to be unbroken.

I was thirty-seven years old now and managed to save up for our trip to India. We spent three weeks in India. We had also made this trip with my parents. India felt like home, and meeting my dad's family after so many years and with my children was just a dream come true. Jeevan and Shanae were given so much love. We visited many gurdwaras, and they learnt more about Sikh history. Jeevan had already written a list of Sikh gurdwaras he wanted us to visit.

They enjoyed visiting Sri Harminder Sahib Ji, the Golden Temple in Amritsar, and Jeevan, bathed in the holy water. He was so excited, and it took us some time to get him back out. We spent a week in Rajasthan, Jaipur, and did lots of shopping and sightseeing. Jeevan and Shanae even attended the local village school for a few days and made friends. My dad had actually been schooled there when he was a little boy, so it was special for them. Jeevan and Shanae would teach the village children at the school how to speak English too.

My dad had also helped set up football clubs for the village children and other villages close by, so Jeevan was able to make many friends and enjoyed playing football. His new friends would come and knock for him to come and play football with them. It was lovely to see how other children tried to include Jeevan too.

In India, I learnt of the selfless service of Bhagat Puran Singh Ji, the founder of the Pingalwara Charity based in Amritsar. He dedicated his whole life to serving humanity, the homeless, the sick, and special needs people. I read his memoir, and it touched my soul deeply. Jeevan, Shanae, and I discussed his journey and decided that we would do some selfless service to humanity once we returned to England.

Cassian would frequently call to talk to them. They would tell him all about their adventures. They enjoyed the fresh *rotis*, loved going over to the farm daily, and watch the men at work. Jeevan and I climbed into the family tractor one afternoon, which was full of rice and would be getting sold at some point. We put some into a bag to take back home with us. When we arrived back, one of the first things we did was place the rice carefully into some tiny glass jars and displayed it in our kitchen. When we looked at the rice in the jar, it would bring back memories of our trip to India.

Chapter 24

A Revised Perspective

When I returned from India, I joined the Midland Langar Seva Society, a Sikh charity that feeds the homeless. Jeevan and Shanae would come with me on some occasions and help wherever they could. They both really enjoyed this and knew they were doing something good for others and had a wider understanding of what selfless service meant. It felt great to be volunteering with other selfless individuals who all had the same vision as me; there were no judgements. I felt fortunate to be in a position where I could help others too and make a difference in the world.

I was enjoying teaching maths and learning so much more myself. I learnt about the 'Golden ratio' and how significant it is to the universe. I was fascinated by how this one special mathematical sequence 1.618 was so important and how absolutely everything that existed in nature, including human beings, was all linked to the golden ratio.

It is actually quite interesting how it connects with concepts like the Fibonacci Sequence. So, let me offer a brief explanation to those not in the know. Fibonacci sequences are a string of numbers where the number is the sum of the two numbers that came before it (It goes like this: 0,1,1,2,3,5,8,13, etc.). This gets interesting when you divide any two successive Fibonacci numbers (like 3&5, 5&8, or 8&13). And what do you get as the answer? 1.618 or something very close to it. That's right, the golden ratio.

How this ties in with life is incredible. Everything from how a flower is rounded to how cell-limes are arranged in plants is based on the golden ratio. Learning about this gave me more of an insight that everything in the universe came from oneness.

At this point, my career took another turn. After working in mainstream schools for sixteen years, I was given an opportunity to work as a maths teacher in a Specialist School. The school specialized in Autism spectrum conditions or an identified social, emotional, or mental health need. I was now not just teaching students academically; I was also helping them with their well-being and mental health. This role fulfilled my ultimate purpose in life, and I felt I was ready to make this change. I would now put most of my energy into helping and guiding children and their families to live purposeful lives. Safeguarding and well-being was the most important aspect for the learners, and the school's vision was in line with my own views when it came to educating our children.

I had also volunteered to be a part of the staff well-being team. I recognised how difficult this profession was for staff, and especially if they had families to take care of, they would need all the support they could get. I am also a part of the Equality and Diversity Group at my school, which involves supporting the objectives of the school by looking at policies and practices making sure there is no discrimination in the workplace and everyone is treated equally and fairly.

I was now working with some selfless individuals who inspired one another to thrive, and I felt truly honoured to be a part of it. After everything I had been through, I can honestly say that it made me a stronger and a better person. My journey throughout my career led me to the perfect place for me to shine my light on others and have others' light shining bright on me. I had let my past go by forgiving myself and others. I didn't worry about the future because I knew that I would be guided in the right direction if I remained humble and true to myself.

I had a short relationship during this time, but it wasn't good for me, I seemed to attract broken men, and I had come to realize that I was worthy of so much more. I knew that these were lessons I had to learn for myself, and grateful that I was able to walk away from them. I sat Jeevan and Shanae down and explained that I was not perfect. That I would also make mistakes along the way, but I promised them that if someone didn't feel right for me and us as a family, they would not be a part of our lives. They both asked me lots of questions and had matured enough to understand a little about relationships.

Jeevan had said to me, *"Mum, you don't need a*

boyfriend. You have us," Shanae said, *"Well, I don't like it when mummy is alone when we go to stay with daddy, so I don't mind; I just want mummy to be happy."* They were still very young, and I knew that I was the happiest when it was just the three of us. I would never get this time back with them, so I had to make better decisions regarding relationships. They were also good at communicating with me if they didn't like someone. They were good at picking up negative vibes when people were around me and would tell me so.

My dear friend Nathan had a conversation with Jeevan in particular about how one day I may meet someone and that when that time came, he would need to be accepting of it. Jeevan would say, well, when Shanae and I go to University, we don't want mum to be alone, but that is a long time away. I was grateful for Nathan's support and how he had delicately approached the subject with the children.

As the children grew older, they would invite their cousins over. They got on well with all their dad's family, and I was able to see family members I hadn't seen for years.

I built new relationships that would be ever-lasting. The main focus was that all our children knew they were loved, cared for, and felt safe. During the school holidays, their cousins would come and stay over with us. I had missed them myself. I had been around them when they were little babies, and now they were all growing up. Jeevan and Shanae would decide to stay over at theirs, too, and it was lovely to catch up with family when I would collect them. Years had passed by, and time had flown by, but we still greeted one another with love.

Pops had also come over to visit from Jamaica and had come over to my house to visit us. It was so lovely to see him, and he told me that if I ever was to visit Jamaica in the future, I was welcome to come and stay at his. He said, *"I don't want you staying in a hotel when you have a home to stay in."* I have a lot of respect for my elders, and when he said this to me, I felt so grateful and knew that the family cared for me.

I popped over to see Cassian's mum and Pops during his visit to England. When I saw Cassian's mum, we gave one another a big hug, and it was as if everything was forgiven. I felt blessed to have been a part of such a warm, loving family and part of a culture that had helped shape me into the person I am today. My life was mine, and I had no complaints. This was the journey I came here to experience and learn from.

We took our final trip to Malaysia to celebrate my 40th birthday. We travelled with my parents and spent three weeks relaxing and visiting family. We spent the day at Negara Zoo on my birthday, and Jeevan and Shanae surprised me with some animal teddies. Instead of buying gifts for themselves, they decided they would spend their money on me. I felt so happy that they had been so thoughtful and kind. We saw the new year at the Petrona Towers in Kuala Lumpur and enjoyed watching the fireworks display.

My dad had hired a car, so we were able to do so much more sightseeing. We were also celebrating my dad's 65th birthday, and my dad had surprised us by taking us to the beach resort Kuantan for the week. It had been nine years since I last visited Malaysia to see my parents, and at the time, I would never have even dreamt my life would have turned out like this. I was immensely happy inside and out. I would often look at my parents and think to myself that they were godly people and I must have done something right to have been blessed being their daughter.

My parents had decided to remain in England and instead spend time travelling abroad to visit family all over the world. My parents taught me what unconditional love was, and I could never repay them for the love they had given us. Jeevan was the one who prompted me to write this book. He struggles with his identity. He often comes home from school upset that he doesn't know who he is. He tells me that some of the black children say he's not black, and some Indian children say he's not Indian or a Sikh. I tell him that we all come from the same light. We are all one, and God is within each and every one of us. He isn't half of anything. He is a whole person, just like the rest of us.

This year he decided he wanted to fast through Ramadan along with his Muslim friend at school for a few days. I supported him with this decision. I had been fasting for several years now through Ramadan with my Muslim friend, Salma. I would only manage four days, but I was proud of myself. Fasting gave my mind clarity, and I was doing this for my highest good. This year, I have fasted for eight days through writing this book, which makes me feel proud. One day I will do the whole fast through Ramadan. My friend Salma would coach me on what to eat and when to break my fast. She is a great inspiration.

Jeevan and Shanae gave my life a whole new meaning when they were born. They saved me and guided me out of a dark place and into the light without even knowing it. They have both journeyed with me from an unknown place, and I know that they will grow to be strong-minded individuals themselves because of their upbringing.

Chapter 25

Society

As I started to help Jeevan and Shanae learn to accept themselves, I realised I had another uphill struggle left to face with them. I knew that there was a point where I had to support them as they integrated with their surroundings. Children are malleable, and these years would shape them for the rest of their lives. It broke my heart to imagine my children being rejected or treated differently. I always preached about the importance of oneness and looking beyond someone's outer shell at home. But not everyone else thought that way.

Whenever I sent my children out into the world, I feared what the world might teach them. Good and bad people, as I had learnt, were not born that way. Their environment moulded them into that. And I firmly believe that there's good and bad in all of us. Not everything is black and white. If only the world was as forgiving.

My children had faced this cruel reality at their school as they grew older. I had not imagined it as the ultimate haven for them, but I kept hoping that they would not face many problems there. And my belief in the values of Sikhi helped me to avoid any doubts about it. It was not until my children got discriminated against that it started to set in. Being called a n****r or told that they were not related because of their skin colour reduced them to tears. All I could do was soften the blow.

At the time, staff turnaround at the school was quite high, so the current headteacher had left by now, and the school now had been taken over by a new headteacher. I decided to meet her and talk to her about the racism my children were experiencing. Her first reply to me was, *"Well, they are an unusual mix."*

I couldn't believe the comment she had just made. It felt outrageous that an authoritative figure would say such a thing to a parent. Rather than trying to solve the problem, she was excusing and justifying that discrimination. I don't think she saw it as a problem in the first place. I explained to her how that didn't matter and how the school needed to address these issues. The most I got from her was that she would look into it. I never heard back from her again as she left the school a few weeks later.

Slowly, a new academic year started. One day, after I had finished teaching my last lesson for the day, I received a phone call from a senior member of staff telling me that they had called the police on Jeevan because he had brought a *'knife'* into the school. Consequently, this was classed as a weapon, and the police would be visiting my house later that day. Jeevan would also be excluded from school for three days for the allegation.

I went pale instantly and felt myself shaking, starting from my legs upwards. It had stirred me to my core, and my emotions were rife. My disbelief in the situation would not let me accept that my son would do something so wrong. The first thing I said when I heard these words was, *"Is Jeevan ok?"*

At that moment, it seemed like I was the only one

346

who cared for his well-being. I questioned the teacher further about the allegation levelled against my son. Knife or no knife, I had the right as a parent to know what had happened. But it was during this conversation that the teacher started to retract what was initially said to me.

"I am withdrawing what I said before. It wasn't a knife. It was a pair of school scissors that Jeevan found in the playground the previous day. And because the scissors were damaged, they are classed as an adapted weapon."

My attitude changed immediately, and I was now livid, angry, and deeply distressed. Imagine for one moment receiving this call as a parent. How would you react?

I asked where my son was and if he had harmed anyone with these scissors. As it turned out, he hadn't. He just had them on him in class, and this incident occurred this morning, I was told.

Everything was now starting to unravel in front of me, and it took all I had not to start arguing with the teacher.

"Okay, so who decided to call the police on my son

without first informing his parents?" I asked. The teacher stated that the school did; it was their policy. I asked if they could provide me a copy of this policy, and I was told it was on the school website.

This just did not make any sense to me. I mentioned that legally the school could not call the police without notifying the child's parents or guardians first. Jeevan was classed as a minor; he was twelve years old at the time. This was a safeguarding issue; Why were there scissors in the school playground in the first place? How did they get there? And where were the staff that should be on duty? How could they classify these scissors as an adapted weapon when they were school-approved, to begin with? Was the word 'knife' used when calling the police on my son?

I had so many more questions. But I needed to see my son before I did anything else. I couldn't imagine what he might be experiencing at that moment. And to be left alone all day without his parents, just thinking of it, was making my heart ache.

I rushed out of my school building half-focused and

jittery. I called Cassian, explaining the call I had just received and asking him to go and collect Jeevan and Shanae from school. He was equally shocked but said he would meet me at home with the children very soon. That drive home felt like an eternity for me. I burst into tears and let out a cry that made my stomach churn.

When I arrived, I saw Jeevan coming out of the car with a sullen look on his face. I rushed to embrace my son. He was shaking and very upset, as he should be. I could feel his heart beating fast and hard against mine as I hugged him. I reassured him that everything would be okay and that he shouldn't worry; he was safe now.

I bent down to meet my son's eyes and asked him what had happened. In the little voice he could muster, he told me about the situation. He had found the scissors in the playground the day before. Looking around, he found no teachers to hand them to, so he kept them safe in his jacket pocket, intending on handing them to a teacher. But he had forgotten about them, and they were left in his pocket until the next morning. In his first lesson, he took them out only to be met by his teacher, who said, *"Give those to me, Jeevan."* He obliged.

"You've brought blades into school," she told him. Then, instead of informing me, the parent, a senior staff member, had gone ahead and dialled for the police. Jeevan was taken to a room where no statements were taken from him. Nor were any witness statements from any other children taken about the scissors. Instead, he was flat out told he had brought a *weapon* into school, and the police had been contacted who would visit his house later. They said that he would most probably hurt someone with them.

Jeevan told me that he was crying at this point, distressed, and angry at what he perceived as totally unfair treatment. He looked both at Cassian and me to ask us if this was happening to him because he was black. This was around the time that the George Floyd protests were happening worldwide, and acts of injustice were on everyone's mind. Everyone that is affected, that is.

I was starting to feel the same guttural feelings I had felt when Shanae was kept from embracing her Punjabi side.

Some teachers didn't see my son as another child who was unaware of what he was doing. They had already typecast him into the category of a rotten egg in society.

I was very disillusioned and concerned that instead of my son being nurtured and cared for as I had hoped, he was experiencing recurring intolerances and prejudicial views. This, I was afraid, would lead to the self-fulfilling prophecy of convincing a young impressionable young lad that he is expected to be a violent and bad person.

Just a day prior, his classmate had lost his watch. Jeevan had been singled out of the entire class and asked to step outside of the class. He was asked if he knew where the watch was. By the time the interrogation had finished, and he returned to the class, the boy had already found his watch. It was clear that some teachers had specifically held discriminatory beliefs about him that they let slip in subtle ways.

I took both Jeevan and Shanae out of school at this time. They were now staying with my parents while I looked through the school policies and started on my official complaint to the school. I wanted a thorough investigation that held the teachers accountable for what my son and our family had experienced. I never wanted anyone else to ever go through what we were experiencing as a family.

Cassian and I discussed what was happening and how we would move forward. We decided to sit both our children down and talk to them about the current climate of young black males experiencing police brutality and unfair treatment. We explained their rights to them and that if anything like this ever happened again, where police were called, they must specifically ask for their parents to be with them. We felt we had no choice as the school had exposed Jeevan to this in the first instance. This was a very difficult conversation for both of us to have with our children, and we could see the look of fear in their eyes. I hoped I would never have a conversation like this again with them.

The next two weeks were very hard for me. I lost my appetite, I could barely sleep, and I had a fearful feeling constantly in my chest. I just couldn't get those words out of my head.

"Jeevan brought a knife into school."

I continued working because I didn't want my own students to suffer. I knew consistency was something they relied on. After work, I would attend to Jeevan and Shanae at my parents' house and reassure them that everything would be okay. I would make sure their school work was completed and spend some time with them before leaving them to go home to an empty house. They would both cry when I had to leave and asked when they could come back home and go back to school.

I knew I had to be even stronger than I ever had, for their sake. I felt so lonely and lost without my children at home during these days. It was upsetting because I felt all this was unnecessary and could have been avoided if the school staff had followed the correct procedures in the first place. The knock-on effect was too big for me.

I was suffering being away from my children. They were suffering from being away from me too. Eventually, the stress and worry of it all affected my health and led me to the hospital. My immune system became weak, and I came up with hives that I had never experienced before in my life. I woke up itching, and a few moments later, found myself unable to breathe. By now, I had hives all over my body and managed to call myself an ambulance. When the paramedics arrived, they gave me an antihistamine injection right away, and I was taken to the hospital. It took me a week to recover completely from this ordeal. I was now angry with myself that I had allowed my condition to deteriorate like this.

The only good thing was I knew how to get myself back on track again and promised to never get to that point again. It took some time, but I was able to recover. I quickly managed to get my eating habits back, and meditation helped me stay focused and sleep well.

During this time, an investigation was conducted, and it turned out there was no policy on weapons at the time. The teachers involved had not followed the correct procedure, breaching their own policies and code of conduct. The headteacher at the time was new to the school, so she was unaware of the past incidents. She apologized to me and retracted Jeevan's exclusion, explaining to me that there would be no police record of this incident on his personal record. I was also told that from the investigation, they found that some staff would look to blame Jeevan whenever anything went wrong in his year group and that actions would be taken to stop it too. They admitted that Jeevan was not doing anything dangerous with the scissors and had no reason to believe that he would be violent. Other children had also been interviewed and stated they had seen the scissors on the playground but chose not to pick them up. They further admitted the police should never have been called, and the matter should have been dealt with internally.

Although I was naturally pleased with the outcome and grateful to the new headteacher for conducting a fair investigation and addressing my concerns, the damage was already done. This incident had affected each one of us individually. Shanae missed school, her friends, and an important part of her final primary year. She did, however, understand why she was off school. She had also witnessed the police knocking on our door when they came to see

Jeevan. It was something that she found very distressing at the time, which led me to console and reassure her that everything would be ok.

Jeevan became more attached to me and would worry about leaving me. I would reassure him that things would get better now and that I was better myself. When it came to school, he had a completely different attitude towards some of the staff members and his education. But he missed his friends the most during this time off and did want to return to school.

Jeevan had to understand that when he was ready, he would need to forgive some staff if he was to have a successful time at school. He didn't agree at first, but he realised that this would be the best solution moving forward as time went on.

It has taken some time for him to trust certain staff members. Still, I am proud to say that he has managed to put the past behind him and develop better relationships with some teachers through forgiveness and understanding.

I had forgiven them about it, too. After all, I didn't

want to leave the school in ruins. I believed in my heart that people could be worth forgiving. I've lived by this principle, and I've taught my children to live by it.

What I wanted was some accountability and acknowledgement from them for what had happened. All my mind could muster was the thought that some mother was out there, dealing with the same circumstances. Only she would not know any better and let her son take on the blemish on his record or deal with exclusion.

If only by a little, I had succeeded in my attempt. The school had understood its error. But that didn't erase the event completely. Their promise of developing better sensitivity training and writing new up-to-date policies didn't stop my son from being a guinea pig for their policies. I felt like they had chipped away at a part of my son's psyche, a part that could not be reattached.

It is important to share with you that not all staff and pupils treated my children discriminatively. Many staff members upheld the school's ethos. They treated my children fairly during these times while professionally conducting themselves.

I tried to think about things on a grander scale after this incident. By now, I had all but realised that I would hold my life responsible in my own hands. I knew my children would grow up one day and not have me there to protect them. We all have to wake up and be the change we want in the world. It's so much more than having the world be kind or sympathetic towards us.

At some point, you have to accept the state of things and change them. If not for yourself, then for those who mean dearly to you. For example, I found my strength in my own children. I had long since decided to let go of my greed, pain, guilt, hurt, and anger. Focusing on it would only leave me blind to things that mattered.

Each of my past relationships had added something to me as a person. It never crossed my mind to think of them as massive failures because I felt myself getting resilient with each relationship. Most importantly, they gave me the inner strength I needed to believe in and respect myself. I saw that my children were the light at the end of a dark tunnel. They were there to lift me through the bleakest days of my life. Together, we could find it within ourselves to overcome life's challenges.

If the Bible teaches us anything, it is that you don't need to die to be reborn. Jesus Christ did not need to be reborn to become a messiah. He was reborn through the sacrifice he made for us. And in some kindred sense, I felt myself being reborn throughout the different stages of my life.

Earlier I had talked about some advice that Pat had given me. I realised I never shared that advice in this book. I still might not be able to. The gist of it is that she wanted me to turn off the TV and radio and stop reading the newspaper. It might have seemed like she told me to stop being distracted, but that's not quite it.

She did not want me searching for answers in desperate pursuit, only to be defeated when I wouldn't find them. She didn't want me giving into my confirmation bias based on the negative perspectives shared on the news and the media around me. Instead, she wanted me to turn off all the noise so that I could find the answers within myself without any other stimuli distorting my beliefs.

At the end of the day, we're all the heroes of our own stories, and to each of us only, our stories are real. We are all born pure into this world. However, our purity is not the measure of something we have had no hand in choosing. Family, religion, race, colour, caste, community, and nationality shape us into who we are today. *Ackee and Roti* is about people; it's about how we all have to eat to survive before we can even think about doing anything else.

There have been times where I think of a particular incident – I can still hear Shanae crying. That day I sat on the bed crying along with her, from my own pain, while ignoring her needs as a mother. I should never have become so weak, and that is when her purity had its first scar. I have tried my hardest and will continue to keep my children as pure as I can. But I know I can't do it alone.

I wrote this book describing people as White, Black, English, Indian, Muslim, Hindu, Sikh, Christian, Bengali, Gujarati, Jamaicans, Africans, Jewish, Irish, Scottish, Mixed

Race, and Dual Heritage. Of course, my purity as a little girl didn't know any of this, and I would have been none the wiser being born as one of them. It was only as I stared down into my darkest moments that I began to see God in every one of us. But even as I wrote this book, I had to use these words to describe my reality.

Words that were created as concepts among those who want nothing more than division. I hope that one day I'm able to write Ackee and Roti: Part 2 without these words, only purity. But, until that happens, we will have to continue forgiving ourselves as we are led astray by darkness.

In our journeys, I have found that life has a way of stripping away our false perceptions about the world and the people that inhabit it. Some have to give theirs up willingly; others have them unknowingly taken away by their close ones. Then there are people like me, who have to have their heartbroken to realize it. And if it didn't happen to me, you wouldn't be able to read this book with these words.

Suppose I had written this book between 18 and 30 years old. In that case, there is no way I could have known just how deeply I loved Cassian, my children, my mother, my father, my brother, my sister, Cassian's family, and my dear friends. I had to shed tears, scream until my throat was raw, punch and kick my anger out, and endure sleepless nights. Yet, only by embracing it all could I cleanse my soul.

From there, I fought the darkness within by introducing light into my life —a little at first, then more and more as I began to forgive those around me. The darkness held onto my mind as long as I kept my ego and pride. Once I had let them go, the voices occupying my head went away. They didn't disappear; they just found a new place in someone else's head. And they would continue to do so until they find one that doesn't know they have strength—the strength to be reborn as many times as they need to become their own creator.

Ever since I was seven years old, I thought the Creator must be a man and would refer to him as Baba Ji when I prayed. When I found my light, I learnt the true meaning of 'Ek Onkar' (One Creator. the Supreme Being), neither man nor woman. As a little girl, I hadn't quite understood that the Sri Guru Granth Sahib Ji -which is the sacred scripture and the eternal living guru for humankind-was written in a poetic way to reach out to our hearts by the Gurus. But I do now.

Guru Nanak Dev Ji's message to us was simple. There are two types of people: *Gurmukh and Manmukh*. The self-centered, *Manmukh* follows their mind and desires. *Gurmukh,* the god-centered, let go of their ego and pride by living a life of virtue. It's a simple concept except when it is used to fulfill one's selfish needs. Unfortunately, it hasn't been safe from generations of misled interpretations. And this is what destroys our unity to become *"Ek."*

I didn't need to wear a *'Dastar'* on my head or be baptized to feel my faith. I just had to live for my heart to come to life. I thank the boy who used to call me a *'Paki'* and tell me to go back to my own country. In his own way, he guided me without even knowing it. If he hadn't made me question where I came from, who knows if my feet would ever have touched my home Mother India.

I travelled from one home to another—some

journeys I finished alone, some with family, and now with my children. When something terrible happens to you, let it go, accept it, and move on. Trust me. You will learn something from that later in life.

We all call upon someone to fling open the doors of enlightenment for us. Jamaicans call their god *"Jah,"* Muslims call theirs *"Allah,"* and Sikhs call theirs *"Waheguru."* I had named myself my own Creator and understood my purpose in life. It was to live in the present moment. The here, the now. Not by the measure of a ticking clock or a beeping alarm.

Instead, I had to focus on the feeling of connecting with nature and the manner of life around us. We take so many things for granted in our daily lives. These facts include things like how the sun will rise, that we will rise with it and that our feet will touch the ground when we do. We don't question them; they just happen on a day-to-day basis in our life. After I burnt my feet, I saw them differently. I had to feel the pain to appreciate just how precious they were. I now thank them every day for getting me through every step I have taken and continue to take.

Everyone in my family has taken their own journey of enlightenment. My sister was learning to appreciate her spiritual side, and my mother had done the same with the Bible she kept in her room. (She didn't think I knew, but now she will).

I used to read it secretly when she wasn't around. I found it so helpful, easy to read and understand. My dad doesn't go to the Gurdwara unless he has to for a function. I asked him about it once. He said, *"God is everywhere. You don't have to go to the Gurdwara to find God."*

He has made his own Gurdwara in our family home with pictures of all our family who had passed over, including our family pets. My brother finds his own familial strength and inner peace through his son.

My children have their own paths to follow. Jeevan says, *"Mum, I don't have a religion, but I do believe in God."*

I tell him that this is perfectly okay. He doesn't need

365

to have a religion. Even if he changes his mind, I will still feel proud of him for creating himself to become the person he came here to be. Nothing will change. I tell him to look within himself and believe that he will find God right there. Puzzled, he would then ask me what religion I am. I explained to him that for me, religion is spirituality and that if something feels right to me, then that is the path I will take. As he grows older and learns more about the world we live in and about himself, he will find the path on his journey.

Shanae shaped herself to be a miniature version of me. She feels the same emotions I feel, and I know we can never be apart. The basic principles of Sikhi embraced her just like it had with me. She even carries my sense of forgiveness with her wherever she goes. Both of my children are my world and my light. I will forever be proud of them.

This book initially started with one person, me. As we near the end, know that you have travelled with me. We can come together as one and share my journey, hoping that it brings more light into the world. And pray that it brings us closer to the world we are all worthy to create and live in. I said this before; I can't do this alone. We can do this by sharing and passing *Ackee and Roti* around to *'PEOPLE'* after reading it.

My dear friend and her family, who wish to remain anonymous, will be buying the first 50 copies of *Ackee and Roti*. These will have a message written personally from Jeevan and Shanae in them. This is her *'Seva,'* her *'selfless service'* to humanity. The funds from these books will go to a children's orphanage in Bangladesh. If you are given one of the 50 books, you have been given it for a reason because we know you will not keep the book sitting on a shelf.

So please pass it to someone you know will also do the same. Jeevan, Shanae, and I are expecting this book to reach as many people as possible around the globe. Both to show that we stand in solidarity with them and to let people know that they are not alone. If we work together as one, we can create our own *'Kingdom of People.'*

Printed in Great Britain
by Amazon